Music as Care

This book provides an overview of professional musicians working within the healthcare system and explores programs that bring music into the environment of the hospital. Far from being onstage, musicians in the hospital provide musical engagement for patients and healthcare providers focused on life-and-death issues. Music in healthcare offers a new and growing area for musical careers, distinct from the field of music therapy in which music is engaged to advance defined clinical goals. Rather, this volume considers what happens when musicians interact with the clinical environment as artists, and how musical careers and artistic practices can develop through work in a hospital setting. It outlines the specialized skills and training required to navigate safely and effectively within the healthcare context. The contributors draw on their experiences with collaborations between the performing arts and medicine at Boston University/Boston Medical Center, University of Florida/UF Health Shands Hospital, and the Peabody Institute/Johns Hopkins Medicine. These experiences, as well as the experiences of artists spotlighted throughout the volume, offer stories of thriving artistic practices and collaborations that outline a new field for tomorrow's musical artists.

Sarah Adams Hoover is Associate Dean for Innovation, Interdisciplinary Partnerships and Community Initiatives at the Peabody Institute of the Johns Hopkins University.

CMS Emerging Fields in Music

Series Editor: Mark Rabideau, University of Colorado, Denver, USA
Managing Editor: Zoua Sylvia Yang, DePauw University, USA

The *CMS Series in Emerging Fields in Music* consists of concise monographs that help the profession re-imagine how we must prepare 21st Century Musicians. Shifting cultural landscapes, emerging technologies, and a changing profession in-and-out of the academy demand that we re-examine our relationships with audiences, leverage our art to strengthen the communities in which we live and work, equip our students to think and act as artist-entrepreneurs, explore the limitless (and sometimes limiting) role technology plays in the life of a musician, revisit our very assumptions about what artistic excellence means and how personal creativity must be repositioned at the center of this definition, and share best practices and our own stories of successes and failures when leading institutional change.

These short-form books can be either single-authored works, or contributed volumes comprised of 3 or 4 essays on related topics. The books should prove useful for emerging musicians inventing the future they hope to inhabit, faculty rethinking the courses they teach and how they teach them, and administrators guiding curricular innovation and rebranding institutional identity.

Music as Care
Artistry in the Hospital Environment
Sarah Adams Hoover

For more information, please visit: https://www.routledge.com/CMS-Emerging-Fields-in-Music/book-series/CMSEMR

Series Editor's Introduction

Music is embraced throughout every culture without boundaries. Today, an increasingly connected world offers influence and inspiration for opening our imaginations, as technology provides unprecedented access to global audiences. Communities gather around music to mourn collective hardships and celebrate shared moments, and every parent understands that music enhances their child's chances to succeed in life. Yet it has never been more of a struggle for musicians to make a living at their art—at least when following traditional paths.

The College Music Society's *Emerging Fields in Music Series* champions the search for solutions to the most pressing challenges and most influential opportunities presented to the music profession during this time of uncertainty and promise. This series reexamines how we as music professionals can build relationships with audiences, leverage our art to strengthen the communities in which we live and work, equip our students to think and act as artist-entrepreneurs, explore the limitless (and sometimes limiting) role technology plays in the creation and dissemination of music, revisit our very assumptions about what artistic excellence means, and share best practices and our own stories of successes and failures when leading institutional change.

These short-form books are written for emerging musicians busy inventing the future they hope to inherit, faculty rethinking the courses they teach (curriculum) and how they teach them (pedagogy), and administrators rebranding institutional identity and reshaping the student experience.

The world (and the profession) is changing. And so must we, if we are to carry forward our most beloved traditions of the past and create an audience for our best future.

Mark Rabideau

Music as Care

Artistry in the Hospital Environment

Sarah Adams Hoover

First published 2021
by Routledge
605 Third Avenue, New York, NY 10158

and by Routledge
2 Park Square, Milton Park, Abingdon, Oxon, OX14 4RN

Routledge is an imprint of the Taylor & Francis Group, an informa business

Library of Congress Cataloging-in-Publication Data
A catalog record for this title has been requested

ISBN: 978-0-367-40877-0 (hbk)
ISBN: 978-1-032-00644-4 (pbk)
ISBN: 978-0-367-80966-9 (ebk)

Typeset in Times New Roman
by codeMantra

Contents

Acknowledgments

We would like to extend our gratitude to the artists and creative voices who shared their practices and insights, and to the patients whose stories hold all the wisdom and meaning. To all those working, visiting, and being cared for in our hospitals: thank you for sharing the power of your life and health journeys as we collectively explore music and health. May your insight and experience be the catalyst for the advancement of the field of arts in health.

Thank you to Anaís, Eva, Jason, and Tamara for sharing your stories. Your unique contributions nourish all who read them.

Thank you to those who have inspired us: to the team of artists, teachers, and administrators at the University of Florida's Center for Arts in Medicine for demonstrating what a generation of creativity in a hospital looks and feels like. Jill offers specific thanks to Tina Mullen, director of UF Health Shands Arts in Medicine, for three decades of leadership that she would follow anywhere; and to Ricky Kendall, Michael Claytor, and Jason Hedges, artists in residence, whose work, compassion, and deep thinking drive the cutting edge of this field. Moisès would like to honor G. [*que ho ha fet tot possible*], and express deep appreciation to Benjamín Juárez and Rafael Ortega, without whom his journey of music in healthcare would have never been possible. Sarah offers her gratitude to her Johns Hopkins Medicine partners, especially Lee Biddison and Ariel Mabry, for enthusiastic support and patient persistence as we pursue shared goals; to Fred Bronstein and Eric Booth for their vision for the healthy future of the conservatory enterprise; and to co-authors Moisès and Jill, whose wisdom undergirds this book as well as the developing arts in health program at Johns Hopkins.

To our students, present and future: the three of us have been enriched by the rigor of putting our experience into words to invite you into the transformative work of a musician in healthcare.

May this book be food for your artistry, your wellbeing, and your future, as you explore the power of music in the healthcare context.

Finally, we give thanks to those whose skill and grace have helped us get across the finish line—our editors Mark Rabideau, David Stringham, and Sylvia Yang—and to Helena and David Ware.

Foreword

Eric Booth

This is an archetypal human story: leaving a home with its traditions that feel old-fashioned and constricting to pursue urgent passions and pleasures, and then returning home later, changed—wiser, kinder, more powerful. You find it in literature and in life, probably in your own family, if not in your own biography.

During my lifetime of work and study in the arts, I have come to see the same grand story in the history of art. There were some twenty thousand years of slow evolution in the traditions of the arts, and then a departure. With some oversimplification, I date the departure in the early 19th century in Europe, with the emergence of the belief—named "art for art's sake" at that time—that to be considered worthy, artistic pursuits should have no justification or purpose beyond their artistic identity. The arts were elevated, but set apart; it was thought that they needed specialized focus to achieve their full potential.

Prior to that marker on the human timeline, the arts served many purposes. We don't know why cave walls were painted in the paleolithic era, but we can be sure it was not for the delectation of ambling weekend appreciators. The ancient Greek theater at Epidaurus was part of a medical facility and held healing chambers for sick individuals under the stage. Native communities around the world created dances not to display individual virtuosity but for instruction, community cohesion, and addressing urgent problems.

The split developed during the 19th and 20th centuries, managing to coopt the term "art" because wealthy and powerful people followed the new ideas, finding inspiration and value in them. This became the accepted norm in the West—art was apart, autotelic, and cultivated in separate (often magnificent) structures. This channel led to remarkable accomplishments like masterpieces, extraordinary buildings, and districts in major cities, new so-called "high arts" traditions, and ever-ascending levels of skill and expertise, not to mention elevated social status for its connoisseurs. Other parts of the world were also influenced by this specialized world.

The momentum began to sputter in the latter part of the 20th century, when the percentages of Western populations who felt a personal connection to this definition of art dwindled. The high art institutions began to scramble to find fresh connections to the majority of their surrounding and financially supporting populace. Art for art's sake could no longer afford to grow in its own separate ways. The scramble led to increasing experimentation to rediscover the relevance and value of high art for a larger, sustainable share of the population.

Braided throughout this scramble of the last few decades is the reclaiming of art for many sakes, the driver of human expression in artistic media for twenty-some millennia prior to the great experiment. The grudging recognition that there might be more than one definition of excellence and more than one purpose for passionate artmaking has now seeped into all high arts organizations and the pathways leading into them. The most famous brand name in the high arts is probably Carnegie Hall, and now Carnegie Hall is undertaking the boldest experimentation in the United States for multiple purposes of their artistic power through their education and community programs.

Which brings us to the path that *Music as Care* introduces so clearly and helpfully—musical art for health and humanitarian benefits. This book offers the guidance that all those in what is called the "classical music" world need to join in the 21st-century rediscovery of what the arts can do to make a difference to their populace. This book clarifies how this highly evolved field of music can come back home to serve the wide community of its neighbors and their needs. Everyone in music believes that beauty makes a difference in people's lives; those who read this book and follow its guidance will experience that power in their bones and see the impact in front of their eyes.

Note the second half of the first sentence of this Foreword—an individual's return brings the wisdom and accomplishment from their time away back into the greater good. The training in classical music conservatories and university programs has never been more excellent, and more orchestras perform at a higher level than ever before. Musicians who bring that hard-earned legacy into the hospital do not sacrifice the excellence gained in two centuries of art for art's sake, they expand it; they amplify it. If you don't believe me, thinking that sounds too hazy-optimistic, then listen carefully to the stories in this book. Musicians who bring their excellence into service in medical centers experience satisfaction at least as great as playing for a Saturday night subscription audience in the hall. They play well, of course, but the expansion of their purpose expands their aesthetic, interpersonal, and emotional satisfaction as well.

This back-to-the-future expansion of the roles of a 21st-century musician radiates benefits beyond the musical world. As musicians take more active roles in healthcare, there are well-documented benefits for patients and medical professionals. Music increasingly finds new places to contribute to the healthcare system—in the care of seniors (the fastest growing area), in dementia treatment, in music therapy for mental health; music is used for pain reduction, for relief from depression, for sleep therapy, for reduction of prescription drug usage, for stress reduction, and many more clinical and casual uses. In some countries, doctors are allowed to write prescriptions for live musical encounters. This book presents a clear and actionable guide to one of the most potent and visible expressions of that burgeoning future—live music that impacts the patients, the professionals, and the visitors in that most highly charged healthcare setting, the hospital.

To me, *Music as Care* beguiles the high arts music industry into rediscovering its bigger, older raison d'etre, by restoring the wider humanity of its purpose. *Music as Care* also beguiles the healthcare system to more fully embrace the ancient healing benefits of music, heading back to the future to provide better care and better outcomes by adding art to science. It is my deep wish that classical musicians, their organizations, and hospitals will take up the opportunities presented compellingly in these pages and beguile their own professions into greater humanity and its ancient-and-future rewards.

My thanks to the authors for bringing us back to what we always were, so that we may find ourselves expanded anew by the journey.

1 From Concert Hall to Hospital

Excellence, Artistry, and Skill, Reconsidered

Sarah Adams Hoover

Music for a while
  Shall all your cares beguile.
– John Dryden, Henry Purcell, *Oedipus* (1690–1695)[1]

Beguile is not a word we often hear these days. Originally meaning to delude, deceive, or cheat, by Henry Purcell's era it had also come to convey the ability to charm, divert, amuse, and wile away.[2] The ambiguity of both deluding and charming exactly captures the mechanism of seduction at work in Purcell's song, "Music for a While," one of a small number of early English art songs commonly programed on vocal recitals.[3]

A number of years ago when I was a young professional singer, I attended a recital that opened with this song. As the ground bass introduction wound around its chromatic slithering, I sat in anticipation, eager to judge the well-regarded soprano's skill with my newly acquired insider knowledge. How will she handle the vowel glide in the protraction of the word "Music"?... What *musica ficta* will she choose?... How stylistically appropriate will her ornamentation on the *da capo* be?... And look at her neon-orange and pink dress! her nails match!!... My mind was racing.

But then something happened.

I found myself lifted from the hard seat and iffy acoustics and held suspended. I lost contact with time and space—there was only the exquisite unfolding of sound. I was captivated by the singer's velvety timbre, John Dryden's text, Purcell's alchemy of word and melody, and the hypnotic repetition of the bass line. My musician's mind knew every corner of the song, and yet it was the first time the rest of me experienced its power. Like Purcell's demons, I was seduced, distracted from my anxious need to prove myself as a young artist. But more than distraction, I felt that something primal was touched—Purcell's music eased pains I didn't even recognize I felt. I made a connection with the song and singer on that day that transported me from a place of insecurity to a deep sense of worthiness. Some part within me was made more whole.

I share my experience to highlight that even as many musicians struggle with a sense of self-worth and self-doubt on the path to—or in the midst of—a performance career, our music has meaning and value for others in ways we may not recognize. The musician's power to heal has been recognized across centuries and throughout cultures and documented by science. In this book, we will explore the work of musicians far beyond the concert hall—in the hospital, integrated into the environment of healthcare. We will examine how music addresses illness, pain, confrontation with mortality, helplessness, disorientation, hopelessness, loss, grief, stress, frustration, impatience, anxiety, fatigue, burnout, isolation—and profound loss of dignity. In the context of so much suffering, there is a significant opportunity for the support and holistic integration of music throughout the context of healing. This is the topic of *Music as Care*.

From the start, we would like to offer some clarifications about the scope of this book.

- We recognize some musicians reading this book may be self-taught or trained in informal circumstances, but we assume that most will have at least some background in formal music study and familiarity with the culture of classical music. We have written with an audience of artists, teachers, and scholars in mind, both students and faculty. Arts administrators and healthcare administrators may find value in our approach, but it is unapologetically artist-focused, as there is no book to date on training musicians to play in hospitals. Music faculty and private studio teachers as well as PK-12 music educators may find our overview of the field valuable as background for planning community engagement programs as well as a resource for advising and preparing students for performing in healthcare settings. Teaching artists may find a new context for creating connections with listeners and sharing the music they love.
- This is not a book about music therapy, but about musical artistry brought to the hospital with the artistic aims of enhancing

and humanizing the healthcare environment. It falls within the scope of the field of **arts in health**. As defined in the National Organization for Arts in Health's *Arts, Health, and Well-Being in America*, this maturing field is "dedicated to using the power of the arts to enhance health and well-being in diverse institutional and community contexts."[4] The field of arts in health often supports and intersects with the therapeutic scope of practice of the creative arts therapies. More about the distinctions between music therapists and musicians in healthcare is found in Chapter 3.

- This book does not specifically address the field of PK-12 music education. Some artists in healthcare hold teaching credentials and others do not. To clarify professional boundaries, we use the term **music making and learning** to describe informal, bespoke, non-sequential skill training taking place in group or individual contexts in the hospital environment. These activities are for the purposes of personal enrichment and creative engagement.
- We do not provide a how-to manual for setting up a hospital arts program. There are excellent resources available that can be consulted. We reference them throughout.
- We reference key studies and programs, but this book's aim is not to present a comprehensive survey of the field of music in healthcare or of its practices and body of research.
- The field of arts in health encompasses a range of public health and healthcare contexts, but in this book our focus is on a subfield of arts in health specific to arts programs in clinical contexts called **arts in healthcare**. We do not explore the many ways in which music has been incorporated in non-clinical contexts such as creative aging, veterans' programs, arts programs in prisons, social/community development, and public health. It only touches on the work in inpatient units within nursing homes as well as outpatient care and hospice. There are many other health contexts for musicians to investigate.
- There is extraordinary work going on in the field of arts in health in the United Kingdom, Europe, and South America. We have chosen instead to highlight programs and artists in the United States.
- There are many music cultures in which healing and music making are impossible to separate, where musicians are widely and regularly employed on the frontlines of enhancing and promoting health. We instead focus on European classical music

culture, where music has not been widely deployed in service of others' needs.

We must take a moment at the outset to consider some terminology that will be relevant to music in healthcare. Within the field of music in higher education, there are no widely accepted definitions of several concepts essential to learning, teaching, and hiring: specifically, **excellence, skill, artistry,** and **professional**. These words tap into existing traditions of deep understanding within the field of classical music that matter greatly to our students, faculty, schools, and arts institutions. For our investigation of musicians working in hospitals, we invite readers to consider our framing of these key terms, exploring and expanding their traditional meanings alongside us. Our explorations may unearth implicit assumptions that need to be examined. Wrestling with the traditions of classical music culture allows us to reanimate or reshape customary habitats and behaviors in light of new artistic practices. Expanding the body of traditions not only prepares musicians for the field of arts in health but also moves the field of classical music away from being what arts learning consultant Eric Booth, in his essay "Three and a Half Bestsellers," calls an "Art Club" of insiders (accessible to "the small minority of Americans who feel comfortable, enthusiastic, and at home" with classical music) toward greater inclusiveness, connectivity, and relevance.[5]

Excellence

Tradition: The field of classical music places a high value on performers being outstandingly good at executing a canon of European repertoire. The idea of musical **excellence** developed alongside and is attached to this body of repertoire and the performance traditions associated with it. Excellence in classical music is equated with perfection and fidelity in rendering these scores. Musicians who consistently execute the repertoire with the fewest errors and most aplomb win the competitive battle for elite status. Audience and arena become backdrop to the artist(s) enacting the performative drama. Audition panels of insiders within the academic and arts institutions guard entry to the arena and determine what "wins" based on the musical culture handed to them. Perceptions of a declining standard of excellence may be raised when performers or institutions move beyond the core canon, incorporate performance practices outside of the classical tradition, or shift the dynamics between performer and audience.

Expanding upon tradition: The traditional notion of excellence within classical music has recently been challenged by forces external to the arts, including decreasing attendance, changes in patterns of consumption, and calls for relevance and inclusion. The notion of excellence in the history of European classical music has historically been intertwined with exclusivity, in both performance halls and music schools. Classical music has long been a luxury product created by and for the elite, first under the patronage of dukes and kings, and thereafter by wealthy and powerful citizens for whom classical music served as a status symbol. While an examination of the evolution and entrenchment of the European classical music canon is outside of the purview of this book,[6] it is worth referencing here in relation to the history of systemic gatekeeping and exclusion within repertoire and performance styles, access to foundational and professional musical training, hiring practices within arts organizations and higher education, and audiences' access to tickets and concert halls. Throughout, we see the tension: *to whom does classical music belong?*

All of these issues come to play with regard to preparing musicians to be successful in healthcare culture, where musicians excel when they leave the customary habitat of the concert stage to embrace a wide awareness and responsiveness that includes everyone and everything in the environment of care. Excellence can instead be evaluated by the quality of musicians' and listeners' engagement, and the extent to which a musician has been a catalyst for personally meaningful experiences with music. Within this text, we reclaim excellence as a more inclusive term that celebrates creative acuity and embraces a wider skill set, as defined under Skill.

To set out on our exploration of musicians working in hospitals, here are a few ideas for how an exclusive understanding of excellence could be reframed as inclusive excellence:

- In *Engage Now! A Guide to Making the Arts Indispensible,* Doug Borwick tackles the limitations of an understanding of musical excellence focused exclusively on great works of art: "What if," he writes, instead of pursuing the goal of being "world class," arts organizations sought "to be deeply valuable to the community in which [they] reside?" Excellence could then be measured "by the degree to which an organization enhances the life of its community. The goal of world class status in a strictly artistic sense is inwardly focused if not narcissistic"; a "more sustainable end would be the pursuit of excellence for the sake of the perceivers (creator/performers, audience, visitors, purchasers, viewers, etc.)—*all* of them."[7] This re-imagined conception of excellence is measured by the quality of connections, relationships, and engagement, and advances not only art but also collective wellbeing.

- Loren Kajikawa states that "the very idea of 'music' and 'musical excellence' has reified into a construct that not only favors the privileged but also cuts music off from the world at large.... We can no longer tolerate a discipline that prioritizes aesthetic objects over the people who create, perform, and listen to them. As a discipline, music needs not only to become more diverse and inclusive but also to come out into the world and help to create spaces for everyone to play."[8]
- William Cheng poses this question in *Just Vibrations:* "What if the primary purpose of sounding good isn't to do well, but to do good? In competitive economies, doing well tends to mean pulling ahead of others. Doing good would involve reaching out and reaching back, lending help to those in need, and seeking opportunities for care and repair."[9]
- Americans for the Arts' Animating Democracy initiative has delineated eleven aesthetic attributes of excellence "to enhance understanding and evaluation of creative work at the intersection of arts and civic engagement, community development, and justice," also referred to as Arts for Change. The eleven attributes of excellence elevate the expanded artistic skills practiced in community contexts to better capture the creative processes and to address the inadequacy of Euro-centric artistic standards in describing and assessing the impact of work within Arts for Change.[10] It may be helpful to consider this framework as a model for a more inclusive and accurate set of standards by which to evaluate music in healthcare and to assess musicians' qualifications for professional work.

If we are willing to let go of our fixed construct of excellence, we release the energy of *pursuing* and *inspiring* excellence, through which other resonances of the word—worth, merit, dignity, and integrity, all of which contribute to health—come into play. Moisès Fernández Via has reminded me (only half in jest) how ironic it is that "musicians need to go to the hospital to regain their sanity." That sanity is inherent to music and is there for all to claim.

Skill

Tradition: Sustaining a career as a performing artist requires the knowledge, training, and experience to repeatedly perform musical tasks with reliable results. This constitutes **skill.** The primary skills of the classically trained musician—mastery of the technical and musical skills needed to render a defined body of European repertoire—are most often taught in school or through apprenticeship to a master artist.

Expanding upon tradition: The musician in healthcare must master technique on the instrument and hone a body of repertoire, but within the hospital, the musician needs additional musical and interpersonal skills. These skills include the ability to remain present, open, and engaged while playing and in conversation; manage boundaries and self-awareness to care for the wellbeing of all in the healthcare context; and listen and closely observe body language and facial expression. Observation skills are particularly important in allowing the musician in healthcare to take cues from others and to adapt (musically and personally) as needed in the moment. Similarly, the musician must be able to constantly assess and respond to a complex environment and its changing circumstances.

Additionally, a musician in healthcare must be able to position music as a source of support or vehicle for creative engagement, rather than the focal point for individual performance. Humility, curiosity, and generosity support this skill and will also contribute to the skill of selecting repertoire that facilitates connections and meaning. And an array of non-standard musical skills are essential to the work of the musician in healthcare, including the ability to create accessible ways to engage listeners with musical selections; present a wide range of repertoire in modifiable, flexible formats; play by ear; improvise and arrange; and engage in collaborative composition and songwriting. A summary of the skills required is found in the text box "The Skills of a Musician in Healthcare."

The musician is likely to develop this complete skill set in a combination of contexts: on one's own, in an educational setting, through apprenticeship or mentorship, on the job, and through ongoing professional development. (You will learn more about the essential role of on-the-job mentorship, supervision, and professional development in Chapter 3.) While the variety of pathways

The Skills of a Musician in Healthcare

Social and Interpersonal Skills:

- Position music as a source of support or vehicle for creative engagement rather than the focal point for individual performance
- Remain present, open, and engaged with others while playing and in conversation
- Manage boundaries and self-awareness to care for the wellbeing of all present in the environment
- Take cues from others and adapt (musically and personally) as needed
- Listen and closely observe body language and facial expression
- Assess and respond to a complex environment and its changing circumstances

Musical Skills:

- Perform with exemplary technique and musicianship
- Perform a wide body of seasoned repertoire with refined artistry
- Select repertoire that supports healing and facilitates connections and meaning
- Create accessible ways to engage listeners with musical selections
- Present a wide range of repertoire in modifiable, flexible formats
- Adapt presentation of repertoire by adjusting tempo, dynamics, and timbre in response to the context
- Play by ear
- Improvise, arrange, compose collaboratively, and write songs

to skill currently found in the field reflects the current lack of certification and formalized training, it also reveals structural biases within classical music culture that can no longer be ignored. Most classical music training has not prioritized but instead actively discouraged playing by ear, improvising, arranging, composing collaboratively, and developing a body of repertoire that embraces a range of styles. These skills were essential to the livelihoods of many of the canonical European composer/performers, but became less relevant over the course of the 19th century as performance and virtuosity increased in importance. Now these skills are more often practiced within non-white, non-classical musical traditions. The exclusion of these skills in PK-12 school music education and higher education conservatory cultures has recently been identified as a characteristic of classical music's white supremacist culture.[11] Indeed, Loren Kajikawa points out the "race-neutral terminology of music education" in which "certain standards of musical excellence are simply taken for granted" is not inclusive of the musical skills associated with non-Western art music.

Very much to the point of our book, this systemic bias has hindered musicians' readiness for work in clinical settings and may explain why a significant proportion of musicians hired in to work in healthcare (including Tamara Wellons and Jason Hedges, whose stories are found in Artist Spotlights 3 and 4) are outsiders to conservatory music culture. We hope that this book urges those within the field of classical music to recognize the exceptional skills of artists like Tamara and Jason; validate the other-focused orientation of Anaís Azul and Eva Cappelletti-Chao, who were trained as classical musicians; and become aware of the numerous musicians ready to be welcomed into and nurtured for the field of arts in health, if there is a pathway.

Artistry

Tradition: In many music cultures, musicians train technique and study repertoire in order to reliably meet the challenges each presents. But neither is the end in itself—the goal is transcending these concerns to tap into one's artistry. **Artistry** is the consummate skillset of the artist that has the potential to reveal meaning, to surprise, and to delight. It is the personal response of a particular creative mind relating to a particular situation, which may open a path to transcendence and ecstasy for those listening.

Expanding upon tradition: As we saw above in the discussion of skills, a musician working in the hospital needs a broad skill set to navigate effectively and safely in a complex medical environment. But it is the musician's holistic interweaving of musical and interpersonal skills that allows her to transport, enchant, and affirm dignity amidst extremely challenging circumstances. In the hospital, the musician's artistry serves the aim of engendering wellbeing. Human connection and the listener's self-transcendence are not happy coincidences but desired outcomes. Artistry enables the listener either to transport himself out of his untenable present situation or to feel affirmed exactly where and as he is. Both are healing.

Professional

Tradition: A **professional** musician is someone with a high level of skill and artistry who earns a living by working as a performer, studio teacher, composer, music educator, music industry professional, scholar, teaching artist, or combination of any of these.

Expanding upon tradition: We will use the term **musician in healthcare** within our book to describe a professional musician who has a high level of knowledge, skill, and experience associated with both the music and healthcare domains, further explored in Chapters 2 and 3. We also use the term professional to indicate that the musician in healthcare earns part or all of his living from a position as a regular (resident) or visiting artist in the hospital. We recognize that the field of arts in health is moving toward standards of compensation commensurate with the skills and training of musicians working in the music industry. We acknowledge that professional musicians may sometimes choose to volunteer in a healthcare setting.

These terms, reconsidered and expanded, can point to the future of classical music as artists engage across disciplines (here, with healthcare), seek new audiences and ways to connect, and respond to the field's legacy as a white, European institution in an increasingly diverse society. If the socially conscious artist of the 21st century seeks to use music as a way to be of service, centering others' voices and capacities through connecting and co-creating, the professional musician in healthcare embodies this vision. To prepare musicians for a role in healthcare—and to advance the overall field of arts in health—music schools must confront their allegiance to a historical tradition that has tacitly and overtly participated in the systemic exclusion of musical traditions and practices of people of color. Doing so will result in graduates with the qualifications and mindset to thrive in the clinical environment. We advocate for a revitalization of these key terms, as well as the development of a new lexicon of key concepts associated with music in healthcare. These terms are found in bold throughout the four chapters and also in the Glossary at the end of the book.

As part of the College Music Society's *Emerging Fields in Music* series, this book acknowledges a number of increasingly expected practices for 21st-century artists: that community-engaged, mission-driven citizen artists are a new norm; that inclusion and access in the arts matter now more than ever before; that self-actualized, entrepreneurially driven portfolio careers have new traction; that technology drives new opportunities to connect with consumers in a digital age; and that markets for music are expanding in non-traditional contexts, one of which is health/wellness and healthcare.

Coincident with shifts in arts markets and arts consumption are shifts in healthcare culture, which is moving away from a doctor-centered model of treating/curing disease and toward a patient-centered model of fostering health more holistically. The arts are being recognized for the vital role they can play in responding to these shifts. In the United States, music was included by the Global Wellness Summit as one of the primary "wellness trends" on the horizon.[12] And the U.K. model of social prescribing, defined as "the practice of referring patients to social activities instead of or as complementary to more 'conventional' forms of medicine" to improve their overall health,[13] may soon be adopted in our country.

Here are the highlights of what we know thus far about music's value in clinical settings:[14]

- It has been shown to reduce healthcare costs.
- Access to music can result in shorter hospital stays due to fewer complications and faster recovery.
- Patients require less medication due to reduction in perceived pain levels.
- Music has been shown to promote healing by reducing stress and offering positive distraction.
- Music can boost workplace satisfaction for hospital employees by reducing stress and elevating staff morale.
- Music programs and interventions have been shown to bolster patient experience scores.

In the big picture of a healthcare budget, music programs are a high-value proposition: low cost, high impact for patients and staff, and attractive to media and donors, with minimal negative side effects. Overall, music is a cost-effective, even cost-saving, way to deliver a range of positive outcomes.

Given music's demonstrated benefits, we advocate for its widespread incorporation into the healthcare environment. This book introduces the who, why, what, how, and for whom of bringing music to the hospital. In this chapter we have outlined the scope of our exploration and identified the key concepts of excellence, artistry, skill, and professionalism that will be further explored in the remaining chapters. Chapter 2 surveys the terrain where we encounter musicians currently at work within the environment of healthcare and also identifies new ground for exploration and musical creativity. In Chapter 3 we address the coalescing of an academic discipline and a professional field around artists working in healthcare, and the implications these developments may have on artistic practices and employment. Finally, Chapter 4 delves into the importance of communication and collaboration as the foundation for music in healthcare and lays out a bold vision for the future of music in hospitals.

In between chapters we spotlight four musicians working in hospitals. The spotlights zoom in on the distinctive stories of their work as a musician in healthcare and bring information in the body chapters to life. Anaís Azul, formerly an Arts|Lab fellow at the Boston Medical Center when they were pursuing a Masters of Music at Boston University, is now a California-based singer-songwriter, composer, and teaching artist currently pursuing a Composer-Performer MFA at California Institute of the Arts.

Violinist Eva Cappelletti-Chao performs with the Baltimore Symphony Orchestra, at the Kennedy Center, and with many ensembles in the Washington, D.C. area. In 2012 she received training at Montgomery Hospice and has played there as an artist with A Musical Heart ever since.

A rhythm and blues, jazz, and dance music singer and songwriter, Tamara Wellons has performed internationally. She was an artist in residence at Lombardi Comprehensive Cancer Center in Washington, D.C. for eight years and is currently manager of the artist in residence program at Inova Schar Cancer Institute in Falls Church, Virginia.

Jason Hedges has been active as a musician and actor in Gainesville, Florida for the past 15 years, playing in rock bands including Heavy Petty and Hedges. He has been an artist in residence at UF Health Shands Hospital for six years.

We also include two visionary essays called Impromptus by Moisès Fernández Via, Founding Director of Arts|Lab at Boston Medical Center. He is an internationally acclaimed pianist who serves as Boston University College of Fine Arts' liaison with the medical campus, where he builds relationships between artistic creativity and health care practice. As a performer, his own artistic practice was transformed by his experience volunteering in the

Oncology Department of the Vall d'Hebron Children's Hospital in Barcelona, and he has since "voluntarily distanced [himself] from the virtuoso soloist figure, having expressed his conviction that individual ability is only meaningful if approached as a collective opportunity."[15] As mentor to young artists entering the hospital, Fernández Via helps build their awareness and confidence in responding to circumstances within the hospital. Here he offers reflections on how musicians may best contribute to the environment of care, as well as his perspective on the inherent health that music brings to healthcare culture.

Chapter 3's author Jill Sonke presents her perspective as a leader in the field of arts in health. She has hired and mentored numerous artists over more than 25 years while developing the Arts in Medicine programs at the University of Florida in Gainesville, Florida. Sonke entered the emerging field as an artist in residence at UF Health Shands Hospital in 1994. Finding her niche, she combined her creative practice as a dancer with her academic and research leadership to co-create the Center for Arts in Medicine at the University of Florida in 1996. Today, the Arts in Medicine programs at the University of Florida are known internationally for their leadership in research, education, and practice in the field of arts in health. Sonke's current research focuses on the arts in public health, the arts and health communication, and the effects of live preferential music in emergency medicine. As an artist, Jill lives for the moments of transcendence that she first found in ensemble performance on stages, and then discovered—with amplified meaning—in dancing with patients in the hospital. As her teachers, these patients who achieved profound mastery of creative processes, not through training but through the urgency of facing their own mortality, have shaped the field of arts in health that Jill is ever driven to advance.

My own perspective on music in healthcare has arisen out of developing experiential learning opportunities in community engagement for emerging professional musicians, first through founding a community music festival and now as one of the architects of Peabody Conservatory's Breakthrough Curriculum. This curriculum incorporates citizen artistry into the core training of the 21st-century performing artist and supports a corps of community-embedded artists in residence, fellows, and interns. In my current position as Associate Dean for Innovation, Interdisciplinary Partnerships & Community Initiatives, I also direct Peabody's performing arts and health partnership with colleagues across Johns Hopkins Medicine to conduct research, develop therapies, incorporate music into clinical settings, and provide multidisciplinary clinical care to performing artists at and beyond Peabody. After a two-decade career as a classical singer and teacher of singing, my passionate commitment to bringing music to healthcare has grown out of personal experience with a neurological voice disorder that required me to radically redefine the value of the arts in my life. My journey took me, to my surprise, from the conservatory to the hospital, where I have discovered new joy in music and experienced its potential for healing. I concur with Jason Hedges when he says in Artist Spotlight 4 that "I don't think we have even scratched the surface."

In our book, we invite you to consider a range of opportunities for musicians at the intersection of music and health—those already available and those which could be brought into being as the field of arts in health evolves. The pace of evolution has quickened due to the emergence of coronavirus, which has swept through our cities as we have been at work on this book. The pandemic has permanently changed arts practices as well as healthcare protocols. It has disproportionally affected Black and brown people, highlighted longstanding health inequities, and coincided with widespread, urgent calls for racial justice. In response to this public health crisis, we have witnessed musicians providing solace, lifting spirits, and offering space for grief. We hope this introduction to the possibilities of music in healthcare will leave you curious to learn more and get you generating creative responses to the urgent challenges in healthcare. We hope you may find and create meaningful work for yourself in a new context.

Notes

1 Peter Holman and Robert Thompson, "Purcell, Henry (ii)," *Grove Music Online*, 2001, accessed November 2020, https://www.oxfordmusiconline.com/grovemusic/view/10.1093/gmo/9781561592630.001.0001/omo-9781561592630-e-6002278249?rskey=TNOVCH.

2 "beguile, v.". OED Online, Oxford University Press, September 2020, accessed November 19, 2020, https://www.oed.com/view/Entry/17166?rskey=SVKTjr&result=2.

3 There are many ravishing recordings. Here is one of my favorites: Michael Chance, "Michael Chance – Music for a While," YouTube Video, 4:03, June 6, 2011, https://www.youtube.com/watch?v=AzxuA7OucaU.

4 Patricia Dewey Lambert, Donna Betts, Judy Rollins, Jill Sonke, and Katie White Swanson, "Arts, Health, and Well-Being in America", the National Organization for Arts in Health, National Organization for Arts in Health, 2017, https://thenoah.net/wp-content/uploads/2019/01/NOAH-2017-White-Paper-Online-Edition.pdf.

5 Eric Booth, "Three and a Half Bestsellers," Eric Booth, Eric Booth, 2013, https://ericbooth.net/three-and-a-half-bestsellers/.

6 I am indebted to the work of the following authors in tracing the rise of the European classical music canon: Leon Botstein, "Music and Its Public: Habits of Listening and the Crisis of Musical Modernism in Vienna 1870–1914" (PhD diss., Harvard University, 1985); Kenneth Hamilton, *After the Golden Age: Romantic Pianism and Modern Performance* (Oxford: Oxford University Press, 2008); Lawrence Levine, *Highbrow/Lowbrow: The Emergence of Cultural Hierarchy in America* (Cambridge: Harvard University Press, 1988); and William Weber, *The Great Transformation of Musical Taste: Concert Programming from Haydn to Brahms* (Cambridge: Cambridge University Press, 2008).

7 Doug Borwick, *Engage Now! A Guide to Making the Arts Indispensible* (Winston-Salem: ArtsEngaged, 2015), 69–70.

8 Loren Kajikawa, "The Possessive Investment in Classical Music: Confronting Legacies of White Supremacy in U.S. Schools and Departments of Music," in *Seeing Race Again*, ed. Kimberlé Williams Crenshaw (Oakland: University of California Press, 2019), 170–171.

9 William Cheng, *Just Vibrations: The Purpose of Sounding Good* (Ann Arbor: University of Michigan Press, 2017), 8.

10 "Aesthetic Perspectives: Attributes of Excellence in Arts for Change," Animating Democracy, Americans for the Arts, accessed 2020, http://www.animatingdemocracy.org/aesthetic-perspectives.

11 Kajikawa, "The Possessive Investment," 161.

12 Beth McGroarty, "Wellness Music," 2020 Global Wellness Trends, 2020 Global Wellness Summit, 2019, https://www.globalwellnesssummit.com/2020-global-wellness-trends/wellness-music/.

13 "Social Prescribing," Culture, Health and Wellbeing Alliance, Arts Council England, accessed 2020, https://www.culturehealthandwellbeing.org.uk/resources/social-prescribing.

14 A helpful research database for finding music and medicine research studies is Berklee Research, Media and Information Exchange's Music and Health Institute Taxonomy: https://remix.berklee.edu/mhi/taxonomy.html. Studies can be searched by medical- or music-related terms. See also Cheryl Dileo and Joke Bradt, *Medical music therapy: A meta-analysis and agenda for future research* (Cherry Hill: Jeffrey Books, 2005) and Lea Wolf and Thomas Wolf, *Music and Health Care* (Carnegie Hall and WolfBrown, 2011).

15 "Moisès Fernández Via," School of Medicine, Boston University, accessed 2020, https://www.bumc.bu.edu/busm/about/diversity/office-of-diversity-and-inclusion/deans-and-staff/moises-fernandez-via/.

Bibliography

"Aesthetic Perspectives: Attributes of Excellence in Arts for Change." Animating Democracy. Americans for the Arts. Accessed 2020. http://www.animatingdemocracy.org/aesthetic-perspectives.

"beguile, v.". OED Online. Oxford University Press. September 2020. Accessed November 19, 2020. https://www.oed.com/view/Entry/17166?rskey=SVKTjr&result=2.

Booth, Eric. "Three and a Half Bestsellers." Eric Booth. 2013. https://ericbooth.net/three-and-a-half-bestsellers/.

Borwick, Doug. *Engage Now! A Guide to Making the Arts Indispensable.* Winston-Salem: ArtsEngaged, 2015. 69–70.

Botstein, Leon. "Music and Its Public: Habits of Listening and the Crisis of Musical Modernism in Vienna 1870–1914." PhD diss., Harvard University, 1985.

Chance, Michael. "Michael Chance – Music for a While." YouTube Video. 4:03. June 6, 2011. https://www.youtube.com/watch?v=AzxuA7OucaU.

Cheng, William. *Just Vibrations: The Purpose of Sounding Good.* Ann Arbor: University of Michigan Press, 2017. 8.

Dileo, Cheryl, and Joke Bradt. *Medical Music Therapy: A Meta-analysis and Agenda for Future Research.* Cherry Hill: Jeffrey Books, 2005.

Hamilton, Kenneth. *After the Golden Age: Romantic Pianism and Modern Performance.* Oxford: Oxford University Press, 2008.

Holman, Peter and Robert Thompson. "Purcell, Henry (ii)." *Grove Music Online.* 2001. Accessed November 2020. https://www.oxfordmusiconline.com/grovemusic/view/10.1093/gmo/9781561592630.001.0001/omo-9781561592630-e-6002278249?rskey=TNOVCH

Kajikawa, Loren. "The Possessive Investment in Classical Music: Confronting Legacies of White Supremacy in U.S. Schools and Departments of Music." In *Seeing Race Again*, edited by Kimberlé Williams Crenshaw. Oakland: University of California Press, 2019. 155–174.

Lambert, Patricia Dewey, Donna Betts, Judy Rollins, Jill Sonke, and Katie White Swanson. "Arts, Health, and Well-Being in America." the National Organization for Arts in Health. National Organization for Arts in Health. 2017. https://thenoah.net/wp- content/uploads/2019/01/NOAH-2017-White-Paper-Online-Edition.pdf.

Levine, Lawrence. *Highbrow/Lowbrow: The Emergence of Cultural Hierarchy in America.* Cambridge: Harvard University Press, 1988.

McGroarty, Beth. "Wellness Music." 2020 Global Wellness Trends. 2020 Global Wellness Summit. 2019. https://www.globalwellnesssummit.com/2020-global-wellness-trends/wellness-music/.

"Moisès Fernández Via." School of Medicine. Boston University. Accessed 2020. https://www.bumc.bu.edu/busm/about/diversity/office-of-diversity-and-inclusion/deans-and-staff/moises-fernandez-via/.

"Social Prescribing." Culture, Health and Wellbeing Alliance. Arts Council England. Accessed 2020. https://www.culturehealthandwellbeing.org.uk/resources/social-prescribing.

Weber, William. *The Great Transformation of Musical Taste: Concert Programming from Haydn to Brahms.* Cambridge: Cambridge University Press, 2008.

Wolf, Lea, and Thomas Wolf. *Music and Health Cares.* Carnegie Hall and WolfBrown, 2011.

Artist Spotlight 1
Being Present

Anaís Azul

"Time to get uncomfortable." That's what my Arts|Lab Fellowship peer Dzidzor Azaglo would say—and I agree completely. If you are even a little bit interested in connecting with humans one-on-one through music in a non-academic setting, I would say it's worth taking the leap of faith. If you are an artist with even just a little bit of compassion in your heart that you wish to nurture, working in a hospital setting will be nothing less than eye opening and humbling. When we are in bubbles of academia, seldom do we get a chance to taste reality—what making art in a hospital serving an eclectic, low-income population is going to teach you.

During the Arts|Lab fellowship, the first questions I asked myself were a little more external and professional: How will I be able to handle the stories of the people I engage with at Boston Medical Center? How will I approach patients? What will I do if someone doesn't like my music?

The internal questions surfaced next: How do I deal with rejection? Where is my hesitation to take up space coming from? How do I listen to the needs of a space? How are my insecurities being magnified by the hospital? What has made me lose touch with my intuition and what do I need to do to get it back?

I am still in the process of answering some of these questions but those that seemed most essential in my fellowship pertain to what I learned through *listening* and *intuition.* I think that without practicing both, we are at a loss to be present. We are unable to give proper care to ourselves and others if we are unable to connect to the needs of the very moment. I know that I was unable to do so, at least the first time I went in to visit patients.

My growing sense of belonging within this space was the greatest gift of serving as an Arts|Lab Fellow. Every day nurses smiled at me. I saw the work environment shift, become softer, more loving, more aware of people through activating the sense of sound. They asked me why I didn't play more often. Nurses started requesting songs from me. Nurses would refer me to patients who might benefit from a musical hangout session. A doctor drafted an article about my work and the effects of music in the surgical unit. I held "church" in the family waiting area for a Haitian nurse and an operations staff member. I played Bob Marley songs for a nurse and patient while the nurse cleaned blood off of the patient's body, all of us buoyed by the music.

Every day, I began with a deep breath in and out before crossing the threshold of the surgical unit. This was to absorb the new space I was entering and to release my nerves, my day, and my thoughts. I unpacked my ukulele and exchanged a smile with the front desk administrator. I'd walk to the only window, down at the end of the hallway and softly improvise, finger-picking gentle sounds. Then I'd move to other points in the hallway to do the same. This was how I greeted the space each day and acknowledged all the people and things that serve this floor's patients to the best of their abilities.

With the healthcare providers, we were able to make hardships into joys. Transform chaos into peace. We were able to create calm and beauty amidst stale walls and blaring televisions.

I transformed too. I became a listener. I learned what my shyness looks like and how it can mask arrogance or laziness. Providing care can be emotionally uncomplicated if you take care of yourself and stay aware of your reactions to other people's hardships. I am now aware of how easy it is to become lonely and how much we need others in our physical, mental, and spiritual healing processes. I have learned that there is strength in gentleness.

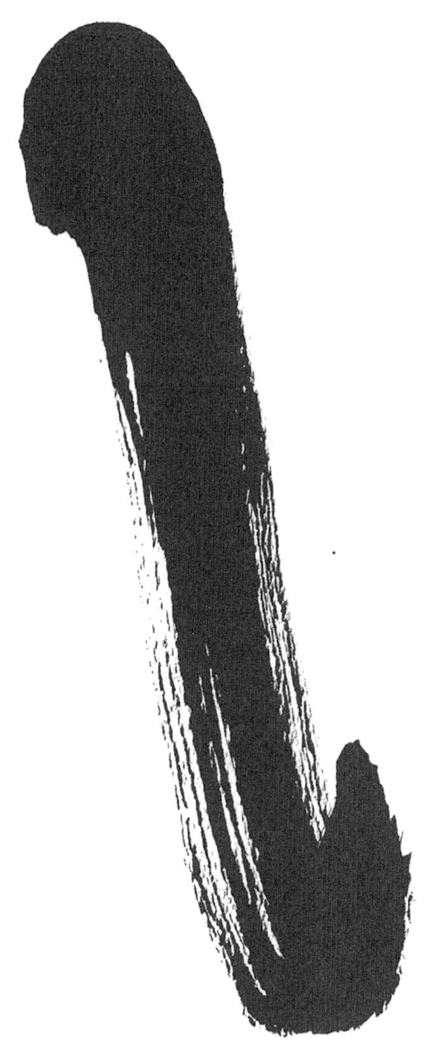

Moisès Fernández Via: *Care*, calligraphy, ink on paper, 2019.

Impromptu 1

Music and Health and the Health of Music

Moisès Fernández Via

There is no problem with music. Nothing is wrong with sound and space. And although we could get trapped right away trying to nail down what both sound and space really mean, the fact is that any understanding of them points in the same direction: sound and space are entirely okay.

I understand that this could come as a disappointment. You might have opened this book with the intention to look for direction. Holding with one hand this text and with the other a hammer ready to hit whatever needs to be nailed down. *Bang!**

But then, I open by telling you that music is entirely fine, and that there is nothing to be nailed down when it comes to space and sound.

𝄐

To say music is good does not need to mean that our journey here is over; that there is nothing else to explore or understand. We still have quite an excursion ahead of us. But we cannot enter the vast territory of sound from the habitual wretchedness of fixing. For our own safety and that of others, such urgency to fix needs to be laid down now. In the absence of weapons, we might even allow ourselves to disagree, and thus expand the dimensions of what is genuinely possible. Isn't that what innovation is about? A lucky disagreement—if not mistake—to which no *bang!** follows, freeing further space and possibility?

I am glad you are still here. Let us begin.

Space

There is no problem with music, which is to say that space has not at all given up on sound. The frenetic squeakiness of a B7 on a violin and the heartbreaking tenderness of a *Bmin7add11* chord continue to be equally held by space. You might be getting slightly irritated with so much blah-blah about space. You might think that this is too obvious and basic. But as music people—no matter in which ways—we should be at least curious about what is actually funding our creative discipline. Do you think music is the consequence of audiences and performers; maybe composers as well? Or do you rather think it all starts with some powerful record label and an almost-kindergarten winner at some music competition?

We could discuss quite a lot about what *is* music, but the real urgency now is to reencounter what *allows* music in the first place. At the most fundamental level, our shared anonymous funder is space. To our luck, it issues a perpetually blank check that we have the privilege to fill with as many musical zeros as we wish.

In the entire history of the human condition, it has yet to happen that space denies room for one of our perfectly unnecessary musical climaxes. More often than not, we are left with absolutely zero award for any of them—we might not land the record label, win the musical competition, or sign the performance contract we think we deserve—but are never deprived of the basic possibility of sound-gesture. Space is always there.

In the absence of space any sound would fall dead as soon as it was uttered. It would be a world impossible to be named; the end of communication, and therefore the end of any possible health.

It could be tempting to think that music starts with someone clever putting together sounds. Then, one of us learns these notes on a page; plays it; applause; maybe gets paid; and then everyone gets back to watching TV. That might be so, but this petty game tells more about ourselves than about the original spark of musical phenomena.

After all, the sensual intelligence of Miles Davis and the crisp humor of Wolfgang Amadeus Mozart are only here for us to enjoy because these masters first realized that sound and space are one; sound simply does not, knows not how to give up on space. We do not need to get a telescope to understand space. We do not even have to go as far as Mars. Space is in front of our face. You can feel it and see it right now; such discovery might flush your cheeks in redness.

It might be convenient to continue ignoring space as unimportant and obvious, but then we have to face the fact that this uninteresting *nothing* can literally make us flush. The giant planet on which our feet stand is entirely occupied and held by space—endless room, equally geared to suspend sadness and joy. Quite a powerful and efficient *nothing.*

You are right; we could disagree about that. You could say no to space, and I could say yes, but even that is again funded by space. Let's face it: We are a sort of involuntary, choiceless space explorers.

This might be saying too much too soon, and I may be starting to lose you. I fear you turning on pages and pages in search of a nice colorful illustration, never to return. You may have good reasons for that. So far what you've gained is that music is doing fine; you should not enter a hospital holding a hammer; an awkward *nothing* touches your nose; and regardless of what you majored in, you have become a space astronaut.

You might need to excuse me—life often places me in ignored corners, leaving my voice no other choice than to speak on behalf of what is not apparent at first; of what is systemically tucked away under layers and layers of conventionality. My voice cannot echo the pleasing comfort of convention when my eyes (and heart) *live* otherwise.

Nonetheless, I still ask that you please join me. I promise there is a great open vista down that confusing path we just began to walk.

Others

To make the journey lighter, let's go back to 𝄋 and replace the heavy word "space" with the word "others." Maybe that clears the air:

> [After all, the sensual intelligence of Miles Davis and the crisp humor of Wolfgang Amadeus Mozart are only here

> for us to enjoy because these masters first realized that sound and others are one; that sound simply does not, knows not how to give up on others. We do not need to get a telescope to understand others. We do not even have to go as far as Mars. Others are in front of our face. You can feel them and see them right now; and such discovery might flush your cheeks in redness.
>
> It might be convenient to continue ignoring others as unimportant and obvious, but then we have to face the fact that these uninteresting *nothings* can literally make us flush. The giant planet on which our feet stand is entirely occupied and held by others—endless room, equally geared to suspend sadness and joy. Quite powerful and efficient *nothings*.]

To enter the healthcare space is to fundamentally acknowledge others. And that could be our saving grace as musicians. (Who knows, perhaps for hospitals, too?) But unless we unconditionally re-claim whatever health there is in music, there is not much for us to offer clinics besides decorative amusement—cute, conveniently human versions of a pill one can at least complain about if one is unhappy about how it tastes.

Obstacles

Back to our studio: In deep honesty, we must accept that the present reality of the music field cannot be mechanically lifted and dropped into the nearest medical institution. Doing so would only reveal how much our field ignores its own health. Like entering a hospital holding a hammer in one hand, it is only a matter of time before a security guard kicks us out. It does not help to hold a violin in the other hand. Our intentions continue to be at least questionable.

To be honest, I stand with the security guard. I am afraid "Music," per se—no matter how beautiful—is not quite an answer to the question: "What are you here for?" That would be like answering the question: "What is your name?" by saying the generic, "Human." It might sound smart, but it does not suffice as an answer because it escapes the basic challenge posed by the situation. It is an unnecessary gimmick communicating nothing.

Every obstacle we encounter in the process of implementing music in hospitals—especially the recurrent questioning posed by security staff—is meant to protect music from becoming an unnecessary gimmick communicating nothing. What they ask is direct and simple: "What are you here for?" We should engage with that fully and reveal an equally simple and direct answer. In the absence of that, I am afraid music in healthcare is not workable.

Beginner's luck

Say we have been lucky and there was no one at the security desk today. We make it to Boston Medical Center's main lobby without the annoying questioning of security guards. Now, nothing will prevent us from bringing the orderly perfection of Johann Sebastian Bach's *Ciaccone* to this loud and hectic public space. We feel entirely moved by a desire to do-good and off we go: *Bach!**

After a few chords we realize things are not going to be as easy as we imagined. We even question if Bach is actually going to work here. People do not seem to pay attention to it; they don't even stop to look at us. And if being ignored was not enough, the space grows even louder and more hectic than before Bach began. The idea of stopping crosses our mind. But how could we in the middle of Bach? Music must go on! Out of despair we default to our learned showmanship. We are willing to do anything it takes to keep people hostage to our playing: Louder and faster; softer and more intense—we try all our tricks like a peacock desperately spreading the entirety of its magnetic abilities as soon as a potential partner shows up.

Unlike the peacock, our tricks are much less colorful and surprising. They only result in the habitual noise of us *trying-to-fix*. We are embarrassed to admit that amidst the chaos of so much *trying* we forgot entire parts—not to mention we made quite a number of mistakes. But the space's messiness must be blamed for it. Mustn't it?

We doubt.

The piece finished long ago, but instead of feeling resolved we inexplicably sink into an ocean of self-consciousness. It all feels inadequate. (No one clapped!) We pack our instrument, but we don't know how to pack away what just happened to us. As we leave the space we question: What kind of bizarre idea was it to come here in the first place? We cross the main door, and make it to the street, just in time for a final epitaph—Note to self: never to return.

Commitment

Any resemblance between this description and your actual experience of performing in a public space is merely accidental. You cannot claim copyrights for it. It is universal in a very unfortunate way.

To continue the security guard metaphor, their cranky attitude understands that our being-a-musician or our wanting-to-do-good are not enough of a commitment to be granted access within a context of care. They know that next to our *Ciaccone* and the endless hours we spent preparing it in a practice room, there will always be a continuous moment *here*, and that we have no special status in regard to it.

It might be very shocking to hear, but whatever perfection you might have achieved playing Bach does not grant you the privilege of ignoring space (or others)—the true situation you are actually in. If Bach ever intended for us to ignore others he would have written it into the score—"*play with most selfish absorption*." With or without Bach, with or without violin, we do operate from the same ground as everyone else: we work with what *is* during each moment; we abide by however *that* situation unfolds.

When I say I stand with every security guard who gives us a hard time about playing in hospitals, I mean I stand with that lack of hesitation to question what are we doing there. And furthermore, I stand with that confidence that is always willing to kick us out whenever we are about to trip over ourselves in delusion.

Conservatories would feel and sound quite different if they were to hire security guards to check on musicians' motivations in real time. It would be so kind to have a crew truly committed to the wellbeing of all at every moment—absolutely unwilling to allow any evasive attitude when answering the question: What are you here for now?

Do not take me wrong, this poignant questioning does not doubt our capacity to be in healthcare settings. Not at all. It actually gives us an opportunity to belong to those situations in a genuine way. The burning questions that demand our attention are:

> *Are you confident enough with your violin to go so far as to care for this situation as it is? Or do you know nothing about confidence and violin outside of showmanship? Is your relationship to music making so clear that it unlocks the collective opportunity of belonging (the bedrock of wellbeing that is always ours, but we painfully forget about)? Or are you just trying to use music and all of us to prove something about yourself?*

Summit

There is nothing wrong with music. We should always come back to this when we find ourselves completely lost trying to succeed via *fixing*—robotically banging everything with our handy hammer out of panic for the unknown. Music is fine. Or we should rather say: Care in action is basically good.

After all, if you've made it thus far in the essay there is no point in building the suspense any longer: Music is care. That is the whole point. Straightforwardly and unashamedly so. Care without additives—before any from, to, about, after, and so forth.

We made it. That is the place I wanted to bring you for now. Look at that vast open vista: *Music is care*. Isn't it surprisingly beautiful? From such an unobstructed view we can look at music directly and see it without the blurriness of habituation. What we see from that lofty plateau, to say the least, is puzzling:

There is no showmanship—no stage, no performance, no audience, no applause.

There is no struggle—no fixing, no losing, no taking, and no owning.

There is no self-consciousness—no competition, no reward, no mistake, and no measuring of here to there.
There is no deception—no shyness of not-giving, and no arrogance of not-receiving.

That is the landscape of music recognized as care. Do you see now why space is the key? Music is here, hospitals are here, but the issue is how space is occupied when they relate to each other. The only obstacle that stops music from being care is the materialistic misfortune of *consuming* instead of *experiencing*—a narrow me-plan that only goes to music to secure individual gain. Ignoring space, or ignoring others and their reality, perpetuates music as showmanship, struggle, self-consciousness, and deception. That is music ignoring its intrinsic health.

You may be overwhelmed with questions at this point. That's good; you should particularly question how this can be a true summit when you cannot recall climbing up it yourself. Your own critical intelligence is most needed here. Climb up to and down from the wondrous summit of music and health as much as you need. Your own pace is always the right pace. But fear not to breathe in the unspoiled new air of whatever becomes *your* summit. It will come in handy.

Maybe next time a security guard questions you at the medical center you will find this exact same air coming out of your mouth, while saying

> I am here to care. I know how to hold this moment to the next one, and the one after. I nurture worthiness at all times. I know how to start, and I know when to stop. Everything will stay the same or change but *will be* completely workable.

You are certain security will arrest you. But to your surprise, the guard replies "Good luck. We have been waiting for you."

Artist Spotlight 2

Both/And

Eva Cappelletti Chao

I grew up in a small town in Ohio, where I was fortunate to have access to a really good Suzuki teacher. But it was rural Appalachia, so I learned how to play Bluegrass fiddle at square dances in barns at the same time that I was learning how to play the classical pieces found in my Suzuki books. The fiddle music felt easy and fun, while the classical training honed my technical skills and introduced me to the world of recitals, concerts, competitions, and auditions. In one musical world I was connecting *with* people. In the other, I was performing *for* people.

Fast forward through an undergraduate degree with double majors in psychology and music, a Masters in Violin Performance, three years in New World Symphony, auditions won and auditions lost, a husband and kids, and decades of playing with orchestras and chamber groups in some of the most revered halls in the United States and abroad. I find myself grateful for the repertoire, camaraderie, discipline, opportunities, and the profound depth of what can be expressed through sound, but am only now becoming aware of the limitlessness of that depth as I share music with people in the final stages of their life.

Orchestral musicians are rigorously trained to play in sync with the other people around us. The technical skills required to do so are precise and detailed. As a result, the intensity with which we learn to engage is exactly what is required to create—literally—resonance. We learn to listen deeply while simultaneously creating sound.

With that said, I fear we are so focused on the internal connection across the ensemble that we are not actively attuned to our connection with the audience. This fear has been confirmed when someone approaches me after a concert to share their felt experience while listening to the music, and I realize that my experience has been intensely my own or collectively one with the orchestra. I have often felt that if the audience connects with the ensemble that is nice, but it has just simply not been my focus.

In contrast, when I play violin for people in a hospice setting, I feel a direct connection with them in real time. The skill sets in this setting still require me to listen deeply and to create sound in sync with the person next to me. Except in hospice, no one else is playing music; the person I am connecting with is in a bed, in the final hours of their life. In these moments I become a witness to the resonance in the room; to the resonance of the person in transition; to the resonance of the transition space itself; to the resonance of their breath; to the resonance of my violin. And together we synchronize through rhythms and vibration—connecting through sound and music, on the journey of their transition.

And when I humble myself in this way, it feels like a gift. To *me*. It is healing. In these moments, we are both engaged in the journey of our own transitions.

I am a professional musician who feels most complete when I am *both* performing with my violin *and* witnessing with my violin. I am a professional musician who feels most complete when I am both performing *for* and connecting *with* the interplay of our collective experience of the music.

After years of practicing and performing, I have developed structures to become someone who can stand up in front of 2,000 people and deliver. Now, I recognize the invitation to let go of those structures, as many of them serve as barriers to connection and being present. When playing for hospice patients, there is no "I" to receive any accolades. It has been my first real understanding that I am most fully a musician when I drop the "I."

Back in the concert hall, even if I'm performing Ludwig van Beethoven's *Symphony No. 5* for the thirtieth time and the audience fades into the darkness of the concert hall, I have learned to tap into this newfound awareness: There are people out there for whom this music is speaking in ways I can't begin to know.

2 Rounding, Sounding, Playing Together

A Continuum of Musical Practice

Sarah Adams Hoover

Thus far, we have departed from the realm of art music culture and considered expanding upon its traditions. We have witnessed the musician's experience in the foreign territory of the hospital through the eyes of Anaís Azul, Moisès Fernández Via, and Eva Cappelletti-Chao. Within this new terrain, we see the musician's focus shift away from their own performance to the individuals and circumstances within the environment of care. We have begun to explore how artistic choices may influence the experience of patients, their families, healthcare providers, and hospital staff and nourish overall wellbeing to facilitate healing.

As we will further see in Chapter 3, however, the role of the musician in healthcare has limits that must be recognized. Music cannot take the place of medical or psychological treatment. Only music therapists are trained and licensed to use music to achieve clinical outcomes. What activities are appropriate, where they are located, and how they are delivered are key issues an artist must understand in order for music to fit within this context. Certain music and types of presentation can in fact be injurious rather than healing and must be avoided. And artists must always confront their own practice boundaries and personal limits, balancing care for others with care of self.

As with most artistic practices, limits imposed by context can foster creativity and innovation. Learning to navigate here may result in a transformed artistic practice or a new professional direction. The hospital, in all its complexity, can be fertile ground for the genesis of creative projects and a remarkable context for authentic artistic expression and human connection.

Now we turn to how the work of the musician manifests in this new environment, but first a few general comments.

Musicians engage with two distinct populations: (1) patients, their families, and caretakers; and (2) healthcare providers, staff, and health sciences students. Music serves as a source of positive distraction, entertainment, stress reduction, creative engagement, and interpersonal connection for the hospital's customers, while its employees and trainees encounter music as a workplace enhancement and have access to musical activities as a form of personal enrichment and professional development. Music programs are designed to serve these distinct populations in different ways, as we will see in this chapter.

As you become acquainted with the landscape of music in healthcare, it may be helpful to organize your observations by analyzing where a specific activity falls within these four elements:

- ***Programming:*** is the activity most appropriate for *public spaces* (atriums, lobbies, halls) or *private spaces* (units, individual patient rooms), or somewhere in between?
- ***Interpersonal engagement:*** is it characterized by *low engagement* (environmental/indirect encounters), or *high engagement* (personal/one-on-one encounters), or somewhere in between?
- ***Access:*** does it take place in *relatively unrestricted spaces* (open to patients and visitors), or *highly restricted spaces* (where access requires permissions, training, health and background screenings, supervision, and special protocols for patient safety), or somewhere in between?
- ***Focal point:*** is the activity *environmentally-focused, musician-centered, patient-centered (or provider-centered)*, or does it fall somewhere in between?

In Figure 2.1, community music specialist Jane Bentley, founder of ArtBeat,[1] provides a taxonomy of the types of encounters patients may have with music along a spectrum of engagement from "music as *environmental influence*" through "music *presentation*" and "music as *response*" to "music as *dialogue*." Musical activities are arranged along the spectrum in relation to the degree and type of facilitation required as well as how impersonal or interpersonal they are. Some can be undertaken with no facilitation; others by non-musicians, by musicians of varied skills, or by trained specialists like the musician in healthcare. This spectrum is not hierarchical—no one kind of activity is better than the others—but rather maps a range of musical activities, each beneficial for and appropriate to the patient and environment, depending on the context.

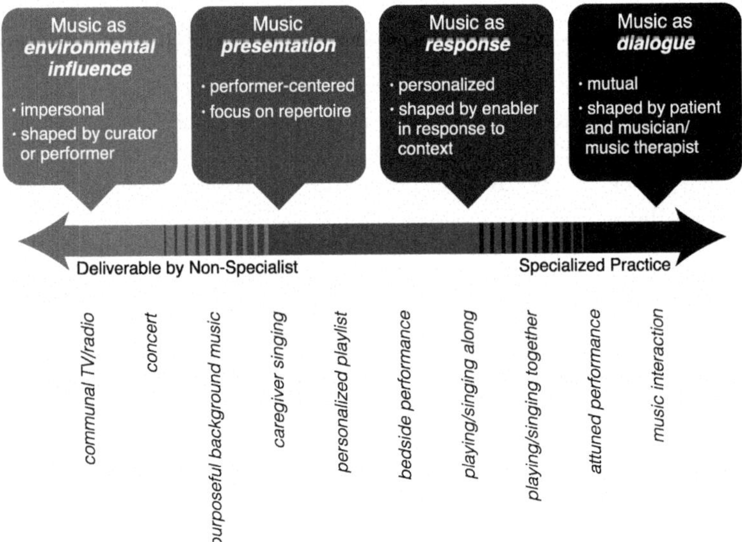

Figure 2.1 Spectrum of Musical Engagement.
Graphic design by Ben Johnson based on the work of Dr. Jane Bentley.

According to Bentley,

> Moving from left to right, the categories along the spectrum become more context-dependent and personalized to the needs of the patient and environment. Because of this, there is a greater need for flexibility, adaptability, and a bigger "bank" of resources upon which to draw from the person delivering the music, in order to offer the most sensitive, appropriate response that is attuned to the setting. Hence, the activities to the left of the spectrum are able to be delivered with little extra knowledge, while those on the right become increasingly more specialized and sensitive practices.[2]

The categories of patient-focused musical activity include:

- *Communal TV/Radio:* Often just switched on and left to play. May create extra stress or broadcast irrelevant content.
- *Concert:* Most common form of live musical engagement. Programming and quality can vary widely. Participants may have little choice about participation.

- *Purposeful background music:* Playing music specifically selected for a given population for limited periods of time (e.g. during mealtimes).
- *Personalized playlists:* The intentional, purposeful use of highly personalized music for listening, based on the preferences and memories of an individual.
- *Bedside performance:* An intimate performance context that offers patients the positive benefits of live music. Allowing patients input in selecting music is desirable. Musicians need training and supervision to be most effective.
- *Caregiver singing:* The activity of caregivers engaging in informal singing during care routines.
- *"Playing/singing along":* A performance practice that claims to be interactive but may be experienced as one-directional. Participants may join in, as an incidental rather than intentional part of the musical activity.
- *Playing together:* Activity with the intention of joining in a co-operative activity, where the contribution of participants matters to the shape and direction of the overall music making.
- *Attuned performance:* Highly specialized and intimate practice of playing for the very ill. Because patients are less able to respond overtly due to the nature of their conditions, musicians must carefully observe physiological cues.
- *Musical interaction:* Musicians and participants co-create, each influenced by the other. Recipients are at the heart of influencing the interactive, relational music that is produced.[3]

While Bentley's model spans a range of patient-focused activities, it does not include more public-facing programs and projects, which have different aims. The range of types of programs makes it difficult to create one comprehensive model for arts in health programming; Daisy Fancourt states in *Arts in Health: Designing and Researching Interventions* that "although continua models can help to conceptualize the core techniques and aims involved in a project, the complexities and diversity of the field of arts in health arguably go beyond" the models to date.[4] With the breadth of scope of current practice in mind, and to encourage new thinking, we provide the following descriptions and examples, in the artists' own words where possible, to give you a view of the variety and impact of their work.

Common Types of Music Programs

Live music in a hospital setting, played by avocational volunteers or musicians in healthcare, is not a new phenomenon: an Americans for the Arts report published in 2009 reported that in 2007, 43% of U.S. hospitals had arts programs, with public performances the second most common type of program and musicians the type of artist most often hired.[5] Currently, the most common types of programs and services include (a) music therapy, (b) bedside music, (c) music in lobbies, waiting rooms, and public spaces, (d) concert series, and (e) music making and learning for healthcare staff and students.

As we explore each of these types of musical activity, we will outline the basic context (what takes place, where, and for whom) and the artistic aims and challenges. While there are many types of programs throughout the field, the examples chosen reflect our sense of current best practices and directions for future program development.

Music Therapy

As we will see in greater depth in Chapter 3, music has long been understood to have therapeutic properties; across cultures and history we find numerous examples of ways in which it has been used to heal and influence the human spirit. To harness music's healing powers through **music therapy**, specially trained and licensed musicians provide musical activities that target specific rehabilitative or mental health goals in individual or group settings.[6] Although music therapists engage with patients and families through music in ways that might appear similar to musicians in healthcare, their aims are not the same. The aims of music therapy are clinical and therapeutic, while those of the musician in healthcare are artistic. We will further define the ways in which the training and scopes of practice of music therapy and music in healthcare differ in Chapter 3 and illustrate how music therapists may collaborate with musicians in healthcare in Chapter 4. Music therapy is a separate field with its own educational and certification pathways, which lie outside of the scope of this book.

Bedside Music

Music is often found at the bedside of the sick and dying, at home or in a hospital, nursing home, or hospice. Musicians can be family members, visiting volunteers, music therapists, or professional musicians in healthcare. Musical genres and instruments run the gamut, and selections may be delivered through in-person, virtual, or recorded performances. In the room, visits with patients can be highly interactive or focus on the needs of families attending an unresponsive loved one. The aims and artistic practice of a musician in healthcare are focused on promoting entertainment, stress reduction, creative engagement, and interpersonal connection, all of which may result in **positive distraction**, creating a "nontoxic event or stimulus" in the environment that "elicits positive feelings and holds attention without taxing or stressing the individual, thereby blocking worrisome thoughts," according to healthcare designer Debajyoti Pati. Positive distractions have been shown to reduce pain, anxiety, stress, fatigue, among other symptoms.[7] Live music is a highly effective form of positive distraction.

In a daily shift, the bedside musician determines which patients are appropriate to visit, enters a patient's room, offers to play music, assesses how long to stay or graciously exits if the patient declines a visit, selects culturally responsive and context-appropriate music for the situation, invites conversation focused on the musical experience, maintains personal and professional boundaries, provides closure for the visit, and exits to continue making rounds on the unit. These tasks require musical training, context-specific orientation, regular supervision, and close collaboration with healthcare professionals. We will explore qualifications, training, and supervision required for bedside musicians in greater depth in Chapter 3.

Musicians rely heavily on relationships with care providers and staff on the unit, from whom they receive information about the status of a given patient. Dialogue with clinical staff is critical to ensuring that music is provided only when it is safe, appropriate, and meaningful for individual patients. Sometimes it is not possible for musicians to enter patient rooms due to contact precautions, if a patient declines a visit, or other circumstances. If room visits are not possible, musicians often play in hallways, near nurses' stations, or in family rooms or lounges where people may gather for an informal, impromptu performance. This type of activity may draw other patients and family members out of their rooms and encourage beneficial social interaction. Music in open areas has the additional benefit of being more accessible to healthcare providers and staff.

A sub-specialty of **bedside music** is the provision of **music for transition**; playing for patients during end-of-life care. Hearing is the last sense to fail, and humans have long understood the power of music as companion on the journey from life to death. Hospices often engage volunteers or have musicians on staff to make room visits and play at memorial services. Palliative care- and hospice-specific training as well as orientation to end of life physiology are helpful when working in this environment.

Violist Nina Falk founded A Musical Heart, a nonprofit that provides hospice patients in the Washington, DC metropolitan area access to classically trained professional musicians. In the early days, she often started out playing J.S. Bach ("and took all the repeats"), but quickly learned that the context required a different approach:

> You may still play Bach, or a hymn, or a slow, improvised series of notes or double stops. It all depends on the need of a particular patient at a particular time, and in hospice the needs may change quickly. They may be verbal one day and nonverbal the next. In hospice you are guided by whatever clues you observe from the patients. They take the lead—their wishes, or if they are nonverbal, you pay close attention to their breath. You tune into their energy and their subtle responses to what you play. It's an intimate dance with the patients; you're responding to them moment by moment. It's like feeding an infant—you try a spoonful of applesauce and see how it goes.[8]

Violinist Eva Cappelletti-Chao, whose story you read in Artist Spotlight 2, shares more of her experience as a musician with A Musical Heart:

> Some of my favorite moments are simply with the "sleeping" patient in the bed. They're not visibly responsive.... The music is not even necessarily "music" to them, which is fine with me. When their breathing slows, I slow the music, or I'll go up to a harmonic or something that's a really light sound, and their eyebrows will go up in tandem with the sound. Then we fall back ... and I'm just playing loops and patterns of sound and triplets.[9]

Falk and Cappelletti-Chao are providing what Jane Bentley calls an **attuned performance**, where there is little or no opportunity for mutual interaction. Here the musician waits for and responds to the subtle but recognizable physiological signs of late-stage disease and the active dying process.

It is important to note that live music is not always welcome in the clinical workspace. Some studies have indicated that music can be distracting or have a negative impact in the workplace.[10] However, many healthcare providers are avid consumers of live music, and the bedside musician may be called upon to provide musical entertainment and support specifically for doctors, nurses and other staff. Musicians often play near nurses' stations or in break rooms. In these circumstances, musicians may discover the depth of musical proficiency and interest among staff and identify additional opportunities to support their musical engagement within and beyond the clinical environment.

While hallway music may provide benefit to those at work on the unit, the primary focus of the bedside musician is on patients and their families. UF Health Shands Hospital's Arts in Medicine program director Tina Mullen observes: "When a performer, a musician, goes onstage, they go on in an outward way... When you go into a patient room, you don't. You go in an inward way. You're connecting with the patient. Everybody on our team has the ability to remove that sense of performance and go in and give their music as a gift."[11] Examples of bedside musicians' work at UF Health Shands documented in videos,[12] recordings,[13] and blog posts provide a window into their experience with and impact on patients.[14] Musician Ricky Kendall says:

> I love the moment when a patient begins to engage in a creative dialogue. This engagement communicates an openness to relate as well as an intention to reclaim an important part of their identity.... Worry, stress and feelings of boredom are displaced by a safe, comfortable process imbued with the meaning found in human connection....I see people moving and becoming who they are against staggering odds, redefining what it is to be free.[15]

Research to date suggests that **patient-preferred music**—giving patients the capacity to exercise choice over musical selections—enhances music's health benefits.[16] Musicians need numerous selections from a wide variety of genres at their fingertips to get as close as they can to the patient's desired mood, style, and sound. Penny Brill, violist and founder of Pittsburgh Symphony Orchestra's Music and Wellness program, states that "What you play is an ongoing interactive conversation, verbal and nonverbal, with your audience. Unlike a performance, it is client-based and the repertoire is fluid, capable of changing immediately if appropriate."[17]

Responsiveness to listeners is essential. The musician develops the awareness to know *how* to start, and *when* to stop, and repertoire is calibrated and recalibrated by gauging reactions to energy level and mood. While musicians may prepare repertoire that is calming or uplifting, their role is to provide support and not to redirect anyone's psychological or emotional state unless under the direction of a music therapist or other healthcare professional. Guidelines for how to select relaxing and energizing repertoire are found in Pittsburgh Symphony Orchestra's *Musicians Handbook* as well as on Brill's website, Musacor.com.[18]

Additionally, it is important to be aware that the musician's intensity and intention can influence how music is received in a clinical setting: Music therapist Helen Shoemark notes that, when working with members of the Melbourne Symphony Orchestra in the neonatal unit of The Royal Children's Hospital, "Perhaps the most difficult parameter for the musicians to grasp initially was the idea of containing the emotional affect of the music. For an elite musician it is counter-intuitive to limit the full emotional capability of the music," which may not be appropriate at the bedside.[19] Some musical timbres and repertoire can be too aggressive or loud at the bedside, as we will hear from Tamara Wellons in Artist Spotlight 3.

Working at the bedside is the most intimate experience of music as a form of caretaking. Among the arts, music is particularly capable of evoking strong emotional responses and triggering memories. This power must be understood and managed responsibly within a given context. Because bedside music involves personal interaction, the musician must strive to minimize physical or psychological harm to patients. Hospital policies strictly protect and oversee in-room interaction, as patients and families are at their most vulnerable, both physically and emotionally. Given the intimate nature of this work, as well as the specialized training and close supervision required, bedside musicians may be called **artists in residence**, embedded within the healthcare team through frequent, regular shifts, often over the course of many years.

Music in Lobbies, Waiting Areas, and Other Public Spaces

The experience of waiting—without knowing how long, for an uncertain outcome—is endemic to a hospital environment. Waiting elicits feeling out of control. Musicians in healthcare address the problem of waiting for both inpatient and outpatient care by offering musical interludes in public areas of the hospital through which patients, families, and healthcare staff pass and in which they may experience long, stressful wait times. The artistic aims of live music in this context may not focus on interpersonal connection or creative engagement as much as changing the perception of the passage of time and enriching the environment by offering positive distraction as well as reducing stress.

The public spaces of the hospital present a performance context very different from a traditional concert venue. Music making is focused on care for the space and the people within it. It may seem like no one is listening; musicians are not "center stage" or even on stage at all. The Peabody Institute's *Music for a While Guidelines for Musicians* states that "Musicians may experience playing in public spaces as being relegated to playing 'background music,' which may have negative connotations for artists focused on concert careers."[20] From this viewpoint, the musician may be completely unaware of the power of an unexpected encounter with a solo violinist on a cancer patient arriving from out of town to join an experimental treatment research study, an emergency medical technician pushing an empty gurney on the way back to the ambulance, a surgeon reporting late for her shift, grandparents walking from the parking lot to visit a terminally ill grandchild, or a resident emerging from an overnight on call. ("Empathy: The Human Connection to Patient Care," a video produced by the Cleveland Clinic, offers an instructive window into the interior lives of people in the healthcare environment.[21]) Rather than being in the background, music in this context becomes part of a complex whole, recalling listeners to a sense of humanity that may otherwise be lost.

To observe how artistic choices influence the environment, musicians often experiment with intervals of music and silence to explore the acoustics and dynamics of a space, adjusting tempo, mood, and texture, as well as lengths and styles of musical selections. Additional musical considerations can be found in Peabody's *Music for a While Guidelines*.[22] Artists may try out different locations, hunting for eddies within the flow of traffic or nooks where music may be particularly acoustically resonant or visually arresting. These might include balconies, tunnels, corridors, or atriums. Preferred spaces are not only trafficked and visible but also protected, so that players and their instruments are out of harm's way in the midst of a busy workspace. Patients and staff are free to move through, linger briefly, stay for the duration of the music, or leave; it is important for listeners to have the choice to remain, as exposure to the music may not be healthy or desired in all circumstances. While interpersonal interaction is not expected, musicians engage with people when invited.

Musicians also work in areas where patients are grouped together to receive care, such as infusion centers, dialysis treatment centers, and post-operative surgical and intensive care units. Research has shown that live and recorded music in these contexts can reduce pain medication and shorten hospital stays.[23] Patients receiving lengthy medical treatments are a captive audience; when playing, the musician assesses body language, facial expression, and verbal feedback frequently to determine whether the music is appropriate or should be terminated. In such contexts, collaborating with a music therapist is recommended: St. Louis Symphony Orchestra's SymphonyCares at SLU Cancer Center program built their program in collaboration with music therapists "to ensure excellent music experiences in a highly sensitive environment" as patients receive chemotherapy.[24]

Musicians working in these spaces are generally required to apply and audition; complete background checks, health screenings, and orientation activities; report regularly to supervisors; and adhere to all patient privacy and infection control protocols. The musician must be willing and able to work under the regulations of the hospital as well as respond to the dynamic needs of the context. Ideally, musicians working in the clinical context will be provided with mentorship and specific protocols so that they know what to expect. Jill Sonke suggests a protocol in "Performances in Public Spaces," found in Patricia Dewey Lambert's resource for arts in health program development, *Managing Arts Programs in Healthcare.*[25]

Recorded music, broadcast through speakers or over TV screens, is also used in waiting rooms. It may not make much of an impact, due to competing noise from other TV programs and patient/staff conversations, the challenge of finding a genre of music that is appealing across a heterogeneous population,[26] and individuals' preferences for playing personal music with headphones. Unless specifically composed or curated for the unique context,[27] recorded music may not provide what a live musician can offer: the ability to adjust and respond based on what is happening at the moment, and the impact of an unexpected encounter with something beautiful taking place in the midst of a stressful situation.

Concert Series

As a major institution serving a large number of people across a spectrum of ages, backgrounds, and cultures, hospitals often serve (by design or default) as community-building organizations. Hospitals attract patients and families from distant locations; free events at the hospital may be the only musical performance they are able to attend. In an increasingly customer-driven healthcare industry, hospitals may consider providing cultural amenities to their customers, either on their own or in partnership with local organizations. A concert series is a civic service that can reinforce branding, influence patient experience, and make the healthcare environment more appealing.

An example is Houston Methodist Hospital's Center for Performing Arts Medicine (CPAM) program, which, in addition to providing patients with bedside music and music therapy services, hosts a publicized calendar of daily musical performances throughout its campus. Center for Performing Arts Medicine's (CPAM's) *Musician's Guide* provides helpful information on program planning for performers.[28] Hospital and CPAM staff view performing arts programming as a way to "achieve important goals for Houston Methodist Hospital by contributing to its patient satisfaction scores, culture, reputation in the community and carrying out its…mission." Arts organizations also recognize that performances in hospitals can be important vehicles for community engagement, as well as opportunities to "showcase the value and power of music in our lives in an 'emerging market' that has the potential to broaden professional opportunities for artists and audiences for live music."

A hospital concert series is generally a traditional performance venue for musicians. Performances usually take place in halls, auditoriums, or large public spaces. They can feature a range of musical genres and different sizes of ensembles, from soloists to full orchestras. They may provide a platform for a touring soloist or ensemble, visiting musicians from neighboring arts organizations (like St. Louis Symphony Orchestra's SymphonyCares program that brought Lang Lang to Mercy Children's Hospital in 2014),[29] local bands and chamber ensembles, music students, and avocational community music groups. CPAM's guide recommends accessible musical styles and repertoire that may reduce anxiety, provide diversion, enlighten, or offer emotional or spiritual inspiration. Concert format, while often relaxed and shorter than in a traditional hall, follows expected practice. In some circumstances, the performances are live-streamed or recorded for broadcast to patient rooms.

Public arts events help communicate that a healthcare system cares broadly for its patients, staff, and community. A concert series can create an organic way to invite citizens of its community inside as audience members and, if appropriate, as performers.

Concert series also present musicians with opportunities for artistic direction, curation, and arts administration.

Music Making and Learning for Healthcare Professionals and Students

Dr. Lisa Wong is professor of pediatrics and assistant co-director of the Arts and Humanities Initiative at Harvard Medical School. In her book, *Scales to Scalpels*, she explores the identity of the **physician-musician** as well as the numerous historical and scientific connections between music and medicine. She notes that about 75% of doctors have at least a year of musical study as part of the broader educational background they bring to medical practice.[30] Some express that they faced a difficult choice between pursuing medicine and music as they went off to college.[31] Wong shares that:

> Many of us had to put aside our deep engagement with music for a time during the intensive training required in medical education. Yet much of our childhood was made up of hours of rigor paired with hours of collaboration with musical colleagues. For many of us, music was our first voice. A return to music gives us a sense of balance, a new nonverbal challenge, and a redevelopment of ourselves as whole human beings. It is this balance that allows us to bring our humanity back to our clinical lives.[32]

Like many other physicians, Wong has found personal and professional value in private musical study and participation in community ensembles. Across the world, healthcare workers take part in musical groups ranging from gospel groups and rock bands to string quartets, choruses, and orchestras. For over three decades Wong has been a committed member of the Longwood Symphony Orchestra, dedicated to music making with like-minded physician-musicians in her professional networks. LSO was founded in 1984 "to perform concerts of musical diversity and excellence while supporting health-related nonprofit organizations through public performances."[33] Composed of a roster of nearly 120 musicians comprised of healthcare professionals from throughout Boston, LSO gathers weekly to rehearse under a professional conductor and perform four mainstage concerts per year designed to benefit local organizations, as well as a number of community concerts.[34]

Another program is the University of Michigan Hospitals' Gifts of Art, which has supported an orchestra for students, faculty, and staff in Life Sciences since 2000.[35] Its 75–80 members are selected by audition, work under a conductor from the School of Music's doctoral program in conducting, and perform two concerts per year. Gifts of Art director Elaine Sims reports in *Managing Arts Programs in Healthcare* that "The orchestra is now used as a recruiting tool for the University, the Medical School, and the Medical Center."[36]

Engagement with music is used as a way to teach important medical skills to trainees and to support the personal enrichment and professional development of established clinicians. Rehearsing together can be used to train key skills in teamwork, communication, and empathy, for instance, and attending concerts can aid the development of observational and listening skills. Studies indicate that musical engagement in a variety of forms can address physician burnout, stress, and depression, and access to the arts can improve staff/faculty recruitment, retention, and quality of life.[37] Wong delineates some of the skills and insights healthcare providers gain from engagement with music:

- In chamber music and in orchestra, we learn to understand non-verbal cues and read each other's body language; as caregivers, this is essential to understand our patients.
- As musicians, we practice and rehearse until the music is not only in our consciousness but in our bodies and hands. In medicine, preparing and refining to the greatest degree for a diagnosis or procedure is critical as well. But in both music and medicine, we are then called on to be flexible and expect the unexpected.
- In music there is no one way to play any set of notes. Tempo, dynamics, and emphasis make the difference between a dry set of notes and a melody that stays in your heart. In medicine, too, we learn to be comfortable with ambiguity. No two patients are alike. No illness in any two patients is alike either.
- Medical students and young professionals who play in healthcare spaces often come away from their performance with a new insight and understanding of the patient. They see the patient in a non-clinical context and see how the patient responds to music. This contributes to the cultivation of empathy.
- Playing for others helps heal the healers. Musical gifts are meant to be shared.[38]

While there may be a high level of proficiency and dedication among these avocational players, it is important to remember that the primary aim of music making in this context is providing creative experiences that support professional healers. The audience and participants here are care providers. Dr. Susan Pauker describes music's value as "[helping] me to do my job. It refills my tank in a way that allows me to give to patients. I give *all* day long, *all* day long, *all* day long to advise medical students or care for patients, and this is a chance for me to receive healing."

It is clear that there is a deep hunger for the creativity that music brings to the lives of healthcare providers, whether through the inclusion of practice rooms within hospital settings or access to classes, lessons, and ensembles. Musicians in healthcare can organize support for musical enrichment through teaching private lessons, forming and coaching chamber ensembles, and conducting or playing side-by-side in ensembles. Demand for programs that provide music making and learning opportunities indicates music's value within the healthcare ecosystem as well as an avenue for potential program development and revenue generation for artists.

Within health sciences training, musical activities may be embraced under the umbrella of **medical humanities**, an interdisciplinary field that connects the health professions with other academic disciplines in the humanities, including the performing arts, for the purposes of improving healthcare training, practices, and culture.[39] Participating students and trainees may have minimal or extensive background in the arts, and take part in classes, workshops, and self-directed projects that develop their understanding of how the arts and humanities can facilitate connection with patients and human experience. Music is a core subject in medical humanities curricula, and musicians may gain traction within a healthcare system through creating cross-disciplinary experiences as part of these academic programs.

Additional Programmatic Possibilities

In addition to established programs and practices, we would like to highlight innovative musical projects that could serve as models for new program development. In our opinion, these are underexplored ways in which musical creativity can enrich and support the clinical environment. These include (a) soundscape design, (b) composition projects, (c) patient music making and learning,

(d) musician-supported rehabilitative therapy, and (e) technology-assisted musical experiences.

Soundscape Design

The hospital is a noisy place. While architects, space planners, and engineers strive to minimize the sonic clutter generated by technology and human activity, state-of-the-art care and extensive safety protocols have created an environment in which patients and healthcare workers are constantly bombarded with the sounds of machines, alarms, broadcast announcements, conversations, movement of equipment, and pedestrian traffic. Researchers have shown that environmental noise itself can cause elevated levels of stress, reduced sleep, and cardiovascular disease.[40] Artists, acousticians, and engineers currently work together on **soundscape design** to reduce and change the perception of clinical noise. In some instances, patients are invited to provide their input; at Snow City Arts, pediatric patients help create soundscape designs for Chicago area hospitals through their Ambient Music Project.[41]

Yoko Sen, founder of Sen Sound,[42] identifies herself as "an expert patient with really sensitive ears [as well as] an electronic musician and sound engineer." After a serious illness reframed her perspective on her work as a performer, she shifted her focus to explore how a hospital's sonic environment could be more conducive to healing. "Everyone knows it's loud, especially for those who work there. We need to create a space into which healthcare providers can escape to establish their baseline, to feel safe."[43] Her work includes an installation at Johns Hopkins Sibley Memorial Hospital in Washington, DC, where aromatherapy, light, and ambient electronic music combine to create a multi-sensory retreat for healthcare providers called the Tranquility Room.[44]

Sen now works with medical device manufacturers to design new machine sounds and address the overall noise levels in patient rooms and treatment areas. In a presentation entitled "The Future of Hospital Sound" delivered during the 2019 Healthcare Facilities Symposium and Expo Conference,[45] Sen cited a study which documented that since 1981 hospital noise levels have increased by 6% a year. Noise, she says, is "a symptom of what hospice and palliative medicine physician BJ Miller calls a disease-centered model of care,"[46] which she aims to transform into something more natural and human through changing subtle things, "like how the devices beep." She acknowledges that it is a painstaking job, where "success is defined by how much people don't notice what you have done." She takes satisfaction, however, in her team's ongoing, deliberate work and in hearing stories of how inviting the simple awareness of sound—by asking "What is the last sound you wish to hear?"—has helped healthcare providers transform end-of-life care for their patients. "It is now not me onstage—I am composing an experience for people," with the hospital as her instrument. In her design, we see the impact of a musical sensibility and sensitivity in helping to shape the sounds of future healthcare environments.

Composition Projects

Composers can contribute to musical activity in the hospital in a number of ways. Working with individual patients at the bedside, UF Health Shands Hospital's musicians Ricky Kendall and Michael Claytor compose songs that weave fragments of conversations and shared experiences with patients into lyrics and melody. These are then arranged, recorded, and performed live for patients and their families.[47] Sometimes the composition and performance are full collaborations with patients, who participate through providing input on lyrics, music, and performance.[48] These types of **collaborative composition** provide the opportunity for co-creation between trained musicians and participants with a range of experience and skills, and can be deeply rewarding for both patient and artist. You will read more about collaborative music production in Moe's story at the beginning of Chapter 3 as well as Carnegie Hall's songwriting program called The Lullaby Project in Chapter 4.

Commissioned composition projects can be used to bring attention to human stories in healthcare or to celebrate a historical or groundbreaking medical event. An example is J. Todd Frazier's (2015) chamber opera "Breath of Life," that interweaves the stories of a network of people involved in one man's heart transplant surgery. Frazier, composer and director of Houston Methodist Hospital's Center for Performing Arts Medicine, based the opera on his personal experience "growing up around my father's work as a heart transplant surgeon and inspired by the stories of all the people who have to work together" to make such a procedure possible. Frazier reported that the opera brought together a "broad representation of arts and science/medicine and general community folks, which was wonderful as that is what I had hoped it would do."[49] "Breath of Life" is an example of the way in which musical composition can illuminate the powerful stories of patients and providers, as well as the life and culture of a healthcare system.

Patient Music Making and Learning

While visual arts activities designed with the purpose of skill building are frequently found across hospitals, programs for music making and learning are less common. Bedside musicians may encounter patients with musical backgrounds and engage with them through playing together (if an instrument is available and playing is not contra-indicated). Skill building over time can be challenging, especially in group settings, as participants may be unable to keep to a regular schedule due to health status or discharge. Participation itself must be cleared with medical professionals and may require the supervision of a music therapist to ensure patient safety.

Snow City Arts in Chicago provides pediatric patients with music activities and instruction specifically adapted to the clinical environment:

> Since we don't know how long a patient will be in the hospital and instrument study is a cumulative, time-based process, our musicians-in-residence have developed various ways to allow a student with little or no prior music instruction to arrive quickly at a place of musical creativity.[50]

There is opportunity for integrating teaching artists and music educators into both pediatric and adult inpatient experience to build activities appropriate to patient interests and capacities that may be designed in collaboration with a music therapist. These programs could offer a pathway to continued creative engagement or more formal study after discharge from the hospital, when possible.

Musician-supported Rehabilitative Therapy

Patients in inpatient rehabilitation often face long stays after a neurological or physical injury. The job of their medical team is to prepare them for long-term care or outpatient rehabilitative services—to motivate them to "graduate" from the hospital. In some medical practices, occupational and physical therapists recruit musicians to offer **musician-supported rehabilitative therapy**, in which musicians provide inspiration and diversion to help patients achieve rehabilitation goals established by the therapists. In this situation, the musician does not set or facilitate a clinical goal but functions more like a musical collaborator in a dance class, providing music of an appropriate mood and tempo to support or lead a specific task, or more general musical accompaniment to encourage engagement in the therapeutic effort. Special music can be used to celebrate the achievement of a rehabilitation milestone. Additionally, musicians may work in collaboration with music therapists, physical therapists, occupational therapists, and respiratory therapists to design and deliver music-making activities that support rehabilitative therapy interventions. As therapeutic music-making protocols are developed by interprofessional teams and validated by research, we anticipate there will be future opportunities for musician-supported rehabilitative therapy. You will learn more about this type of interprofessional collaboration in Artist Spotlight 4 and in Chapter 4.

Technology-assisted Musical Experiences

The 2020 Global Wellness Summit identified **wellness music** as one of ten new wellness trends, and profiled numerous applications and products that aim to facilitate healing through curated sounds and music.[51] Described by Global Wellness Director of Research Beth McGroarty as "generative music apps and streaming services that create tailor-made, always-adapting soundscapes, using algorithms and...biofeedback, to improve...wellbeing," wellness music appears to be expanding rapidly. Smart phone or tablet applications are widely available, inexpensive, and efficient; they can be used to increase the frequency and duration of exposure to music to magnify its positive effects. As technology is harnessed to deliver music's healing powers not only within the hospital but in daily life, entrepreneurial musicians would be wise to study the wellness music trend and current products on the market to develop their own high-quality, evidence-based applications.

When live music is not appropriate or available, care providers or hospital staff may facilitate the intentional use of recorded music to help patients manage symptoms and reconnect with a greater sense of self. This is called **music medicine**. Staff without any musical training can assist patients with creating individual **personalized playlists** of their favorite recorded music.[52] In general, music medicine has been found to be less effective than music therapy interventions, due in part to lack of interpersonal connection.[53] Bedside musicians may also enhance the benefits of music medicine through interactive activities such as facilitating personal playlists, recommending new musical selections, and assembling playlists of repertoire they have shared in room visits. In this way, the relationship between patient and musician extends beyond the bedside visit. By working on playlists together, musicians also gather information about a patient's musical preferences and can return with repertoire responsive to their interests. Active listening together can lead to informal learning about musical form and style. The activity of creating playlists can also substitute for live music if the patient requires safety precautions that prohibit musicians from playing their instruments in-room.

For patients in isolation or in hospitals without access to live musicians, applications that build digital community through music can help combat loneliness. An example is Bedrock, an asynchronous online music festival where artists perform in bed to express solidarity with pediatric cancer patients.[54] MyMusicRx, the organization that hosts Bedrock, created a Q&A format where famous artists make themselves available to respond to patients' questions about their music. MyMusicRx also has a feature that allows users to find and choose music videos based on what mood they want to feel; they can select from "adventurous, calm, connected, excited, happy, or strong."[55]

Additionally, streaming technology and web platforms can be used to broadcast live or pre-recorded musical events, allowing all patients (as well as healthcare staff unable to leave their units) access to performances. This is relatively common practice in pediatric hospitals. Video chat platforms can be used for musical interactions or music lessons—many arts in health programs have recently pivoted to using videoconferencing applications on in-room tablet devices. As healthcare has moved rapidly into telemedicine, it has become clear that virtual interactions provide viable ways for patients to engage with musicians.

Bringing musicians into the healthcare environment requires infrastructure, training, and supervision. To ensure quality as well as the wellbeing and safety of all involved, we support the move toward employing professional, trained artists and professionalizing the field of arts in health through research, academic training, and certification. However, the desire for music within hospitals often exceeds an institution's resources. Both professional artists and avocational volunteers can be part of a viable program design if they have different arenas of practice; volunteer soloists and ensembles may be suitable for performance in public situations including lobbies or performance halls, where they have little to no direct patient contact, encounter fewer medical/safety restrictions, and are accompanied by hospital staff or arts administrators. Performances by guest artists who make only occasional visits to a hospital as well as concerts by musically active healthcare staff may also fit in this category. Conversely, trained musicians in healthcare are equipped to undertake work in inpatient care areas where personal interaction takes place, ongoing supervision is required, and the musician is unescorted. These circumstances pertain particularly to bedside musicians.

As we have seen in this chapter, musicians moving into an arena of healthcare confront boundaries, limitations, and challenges that must be addressed. Yet we have heard in the Artist Spotlights and elsewhere that music can have a profound impact on patients, healthcare providers, and the hospital environment—and on the musicians themselves. We have now set the stage for Chapter 3, where we will dive more deeply into the growing field of arts in health and the scope of practice, qualifications, and preparation of musicians in healthcare.

Notes

1 "What Artbeat Does," Artbeat, https://artbeatmusic.org/ (accessed 2020).
2 Jane Bentley, email message to author, September 30, 2020.
3 Jane Bentley, email message to author, September 30, 2020.
4 Daisy Fancourt, *Arts in Health: Designing and Researching Interventions* (Oxford: Oxford University Press, 2016), 71. Fancourt provides three additional models that may be helpful for conceptual framing.
5 State of the Field Committee, *State of the Field Report: Arts in Healthcare 2009* (Washington, DC: Society for the Arts in Healthcare, 2009), 4–5, https://www.americansforthearts.org/sites/default/files/ArtsInHealthcare_0.pdf.
6 "What is Music Therapy?" American Music Therapy Association, American Music Therapy Association, 1998–2020, https://www.musictherapy.org/about/musictherapy/.
7 Debajyoti Pati, "Positive Distractions," Healthcare Design, Emerald X, March 11 2010, https://www.healthcaredesignmagazine.com/trends/architecture/positive-distractions/.
8 Nina Falk, interview with author, March 5, 2020.
9 "An Interview with Eva Cappelleti-Chao," A Musical Heart, November 16, 2017, https://amusicalheart.org/eva-cappelletti-chao-interview/.

10 Jill Sonke, Virginia Pesata, Lauren Arce, Ferol P. Carytsas, Kristen Zemina, and Christine Jokisch, "The Effects of Arts-in-medicine Programming on the Medical-surgical Environment," *Arts & Health: An International Journal for Research, Policy and Practice* 7, no. 1 (2015): 27–41. See also Constanza Preti and Graham F Welch, "The Inherent Challenges in Creative Musical Performance in a Paediatric Hospital Setting," *Psychology of Music* 41, no. 5 (2012): 647–654.

11 Natalie Roo and Meredith Sheldon, "Tiny Beds, Big Impact," *WUFT News*, April 26, 2018, https://www.wuft.org/news/tiny-beds-big-impact/.

12 "Artists in the Hospital Video Series," UF Health Shands Arts in Medicine, University of Florida Health, 2020, https://artsinmedicine.ufhealth.org/2019/08/29/artists-in-the-hospital-video-series/ and "Tiny Bed Sessions with Musicians in Residence," UF Health Shands Arts in Medicine, University of Florida Health, 2020, https://artsinmedicine.ufhealth.org/tiny-bed-sessions/tiny-bed-sessions-with-artists-in-residence/.

13 Ricky Kendall, "Thankful for Love," SoundCloud audio, 23:11, March 27 2020, https://soundcloud.com/shandsaim/sets/thankful-for-love.

14 "Artist's Journals," UF Health Shands Arts in Medicine, University of Florida Health, 2020, https://artsinmedicine.ufhealth.org/artists-journals/.

15 Ricky Kendall, "Decisions," UF Health Shands Arts in Medicine, University of Florida Health, 2019, https://artsinmedicine.ufhealth.org/2019/08/29/rickys-blog-post-2/.

16 Cheryl Dileo, *Music Therapy and Medicine: Theoretical and Clinical Applications* (Silver Spring: American Music Therapy Association, 1999). See also Lacey Reimnitz and Michael J Silverman. "A Randomized Pilot Study of Music Therapy in the Form of Patient-preferred Live Music on Fatigue, Energy and Pain in Hospitalized Adult Oncology Patients on a Blood and Marrow Transplant Unit," *Arts & Health* 12, no. 2 (2020), 154–168.

17 Penny Brill, email message to author, May 16, 2020.

18 Penny Brill, Elaine Abbott, Deborah Benkovitz Williams, Gloria Mou, and Jessi Ryan, *Musicians Handbook*, https://wellness.pittsburghsymphony.org/. http://wellness.pittsburghsymphony.org/wp-content/uploads/2016/10/Musicians-Handbook_Accessible-PDF.pdf. See also Brill's website, Musacor: https://musacor.com/.

19 Helen Shoemark, "Sweet Melodies: Combining the Talents and Knowledge of Music Therapy and Elite Musicianship," *Voices: A World Forum for Music Therapy* 9, no. 2 (2009).

20 The Peabody Institute, *Music for a While Guidelines for Musicians*, (Baltimore: Johns Hopkins Peabody Institute 2020), 4, https://peabody.jhu.edu/wp-content/uploads/2020/10/Music-for-a-While-Guidelines-2020.pdf.

21 Cleveland Clinic, "Empathy: The Human Connection to Patient Care," YouTube Video, 4:23, February 27, 2013, https://www.youtube.com/watch?v=cDDWvj_q-o8.

22 The Peabody Institute, *Music for a While Guidelines for Musicians.*

23 M. Soledad Cepeda, Daniel B. Carr, Joseph Lau, and Hernando Alvarez, "Music for Pain Relief," *Cochrane Database of Systematic Reviews* 2 (2006).

24 "SymphonyCares at SLU Cancer Center," St. Louis Symphony Orchestra, St. Louis Symphony Orchestra, 2020, https://www.slso.org/en/com/in-the-community/symphonycares/slu-cancer-center/.
25 Jill Sonke, "Performances in Public Spaces," in *Managing Arts Programs in Healthcare*, ed. Patricia Dewey Lambert (London: Routledge, 2016), 117–118.
26 Choice of recorded music in a specific context matters and can be a powerful cultural signifier: recorded classical music has been shown to be an effective deterrent to loitering/gathering in urban public spaces and can reduce crime. See Theodore Gioia, "Bach at the Burger King," *Los Angeles Review of Books*, May 17, 2018, https://lareviewofbooks.org/article/bach-at-the-burger-king/, Lily E. Hirsch, *Music in American Crime Prevention and Punishment* (Ann Arbor: University of Michigan Press, 2012), and Scott Timberg, "Halt, or I'll play Vivaldi!," Los Angeles Times, Los Angeles Times, February 13, 2005, https://www.latimes.com/archives/la-xpm-2005-feb-13-ca-musichurts13-story.html. In the healthcare setting, we advocate for music's attractive rather than repellant potentiality.
27 Vera Brandes cites an example of an acoustic solution through musical composition:

> The noise problem [endemic to clinical workspaces and corridors] can be ameliorated by the implementation of an acoustic "antidote" involving specially composed audio programs that "surround" the typical noises and signals emanating from equipment and operative procedures with gentle harmonies and quiet natural sounds….This "sleight of hand" produces a state of quiet that, in the most literal sense of the word, was previously unheard.

Vera Brandes, "Music as a Medicine: incorporating music into standard hospital care," in *Music that Works*, ed. Roland Haas and Vera Brandes (New York: SpringerWienNewYork, 2009), 330.
28 Center for Performing Arts Medicine, *A Guide to Performing as Part of the Margaret Alkek Williams Crain Garden Performance Series* (Houston: Houston Methodist Hospital, 2016), https://www.houstonmethodist.org/~/media/pdf/hr/MusiciansGuideFINAL.ashx?la=en%C2%A0.
29 "Concert Pianist Inspires Through Music at Hospital, Symphony Gala," *St. Louis Public Radio*, October 17, 2014, https://news.stlpublicradio.org/arts/2014-10-17/concert-pianist-inspires-through-music-at-hospital-symphony-gala.
30 Lisa Wong, *Scales to Scalpels* (New York: Pegasus Books, 2012), 43.
31 The desire to continue serious music study while moving towards a career in medicine no doubt has contributed to the rise in interest in double degree programs at universities.
32 Lisa Wong, email message to author, February 17, 2020.
33 Ann Drinan, "The Longwood Symphony: An Interview with Lisa Wong, M.D.," Institute for Music Leadership, Eastman School of Music, Polyphonic Archive, 2012, https://iml.esm.rochester.edu/polyphonic-archive/article/the-longwood-symphony-an-interview-with-lisa-wong-m-d/.
34 See Lisa Wong, *Scales to Scalpels* for a history of the development of the Longwood Symphony Orchestra.

35 "Gifts of Art Life Sciences Orchestra," Michigan Medicine, Regents of the University of Michigan, 2013, http://lso.med.umich.edu/about/.
36 Lynn Kable, "Using the Arts to Care for Caregivers," in *Managing Arts Programs in Healthcare*, ed. Patricia Dewey Lambert (London and New York: Routledge, 2016), 239–240.
37 Clare O'Callaghan and Lucanne Magill, "Effect of Music Therapy on Oncological Staff Bystanders: A Substantive Grounded Theory," *Palliative & Support Care* 7, no. 2 (2009): 219–228. Darlene M. Brooks, Joke Bradt, Lillian Eyre, and Andrea Hunt, "Creative Approaches for Reducing Burnout in Medical Personnel," *The Arts in Psychotherapy* 37, no. 3 (2010): 255–263. Barry Bittman, Karl T. Bruhn, Christine Stevens, James Westengard, and Paul O Umbach, "Recreational Music-making: A Cost-effective Group Interdisciplinary Strategy for Reducing Burnout and Improving Mood States in Long-term Care Workers," *Advances in Mind-Body Medicine* 19, no. 3–4 (2003): 4–15.
38 Lisa Wong, email message to author, September 30, 2020.
39 See Susan E. Pories, Sorbarikor Piawah, Gregory A. Abel, Sayukta Mullangi, Jennifer Doyle and Joel T. Katz, "What is the Role of the Arts in Medical Education and Patient Care? A Survey-based Qualitative Study," *Journal of Medical Humanities* 39, no. 4 (2018): 431–445 for data collected at Harvard Medical School on interest in and engagement with the arts.
40 Jesper J. Alvarsson, Stefan Wiens, and Mats E Nilsson, "Stress Recovery during Exposure to Nature Sound and Environmental Noise," *International Journal of Environmental Research and Public Health* 7, no. 3 (2010): 1036–1046. Greg Watts, Amir Khan, and Rob Pheasant, "Influence of Soundscape and Interior Design on Anxiety and Perceived Tranquility of Patients in a Healthcare Setting," *Applied Acoustics* 104 (2016): 135–141.
41 Snow City Arts, "The Ambient Project," released September 8, 2015, digitally released on Bandcamp, https://snowcityarts.bandcamp.com/album/the-ambient-project.
42 "About Sen Sound," Sen Sound, no publisher, accessed 2020, http://www.sensound.space/new-page.
43 Yoko Sen, interview with author, January 23, 2020.
44 Bonny Slater, "Sound Health: The Tranquility Room," GenslerOnCities, Gensler, 2016, http://www.gensleron.com/cities/2018/2/6/sound-health-the-tranquility-room.html.
45 Author's notes from keynote talk from Yoko Sen, "The Future of Hospital Sound," Healthcare Facilities Symposium and Expo Conference, Austin, TX, September 17, 2019.
46 BJ Miller, 2015, "What Really Matters at the End of Life," Filmed March 2015, TED video, 18:39, https://www.ted.com/talks/bj_miller_what_really_matters_at_the_end_of_life/reading-list?referrer=playlist-505.
47 Ricky Kendall, "Thankful for Love," SoundCloud audio, Track 1, 2:55, March 27 2020, https://soundcloud.com/shandsaim/sets/thankful-for-love. See also Ricky Kendall, "Interdisciplinary Connection," UF Health Shands Arts in Medicine, University of Florida Health, 2019, https://artsinmedicine.ufhealth.org/2019/08/29/rickys-blog-post-3/.

48 Ricky Kendall, "Jamal," UF Health Shands Arts in Medicine, University of Florida Health, 2019, https://artsinmedicine.ufhealth.org/2019/08/29/rickys-blog-post-4/. See also Jamal Davis and Ricky Kendall, "Jamal Davis and Ricky Kendall Cover 'Golden Train' @ Shands Hospital," YouTube Video, 3:23, May 19, 2015, https://www.youtube.com/watch?v=72GX-h4a9i8#action=share.
49 Todd Frazier, email message to author, January 8, 2020.
50 "Our Programs," Snow City Arts, 2016, http://www.snowcityarts.org/what_we_do/ourprogram/.
51 Beth McGroarty, "Wellness Music," 2020 Wellness Trends, 2020 Global Wellness Summit, 2020, https://www.globalwellnesssummit.com/2020-global-wellness-trends/wellness-music/.
52 Cheryl DiLeo, *Music Therapy and Medicine: Theoretical and Clinical Approaches* (Silver Spring: American Music Therapy Association, 1999), 4.
53 Cheryl Dileo and Joke Bradt, "On Creating the Discipline, Profession, and Evidence in the Field of Arts and Healthcare," *Arts & Health* 1, no. 2 (2009): 175. See also Joke Bradt, Noah Potvin, Amy Kesslick, Minjung Shim, Donna Radl, Emily Shriver, Edward J. Gracely and Lydia Komarnicky-Kocher, "The Impact of Music Therapy versus Music Medicine on Psychological Outcomes and Pain in Cancer Patients: A Mixed Methods Study," *Supportive Care in Care Cancer* (2015) 23, 1261–1271.
54 Andy Kahn, "Ron Artis II Performs 'Light the Way' for MyMusicRx Bedstock 2019," Jambase, Jambase, July 22, 2019, https://www.jambase.com/article/ron-artis-ii-light-the-way-bedstock-video. See also "MyMusicRx," Children's Cancer Association, Children's Cancer Association, 2020, https://joyrx.org/programs/mymusicrx/.
55 "Listen," MyMusicRx, Children's Cancer Association, Children's Cancer Association, 2020, https://mymusicrx.org/listen/. Note the button in the top center with the label "Choose Your Mood," which allows a user to select music by mood.

Bibliography

"About – Sen Sound." Sen Sound. Accessed 2020. http://www.sensound.space/new-page

Alvarsson, Jesper J., Stefan Wiens, and Mats E. Nilsson. "Stress Recovery during Exposure to Nature Sound and Environmental Noise." *International Journal of Environmental Research and Public Health* 7, no. 3 (2010): 1036–1046.

"An Interview with Eva Cappelleti-Chao." A Musical Heart. A Musical Heart. November 16 2017. https://amusicalheart.org/eva-cappelletti-chao-interview/.

"Artists in the Hospital Video Series." UF Health Shands Arts in Medicine. University of Florida Health. 2020. https://artsinmedicine.ufhealth.org/2019/08/29/artists-in-the-hospital-video-series/.

"Artist's Journal." UF Health Shands Arts in Medicine. University of Florida Health. 2020. https://artsinmedicine.ufhealth.org/artists-journals/.

Bittman, Barry, Karl T. Bruhn, Christine Stevens, James Westengard, and Paul O. Umbach. "Recreational Music-making: A Cost-Effective Group Interdisciplinary Strategy for Reducing Burnout and Improving Mood States in Long-term Care Workers." *Advances in Mind-Body Medicine* 19, no. 3–4 (2003): 4–15.

Bradt, Joke, Noah Potvin, Amy Kesslick, Minjung Shim, Donna Radl, Emily Shriver, Edward J. Gracely, and Lydia Komarnicky-Kocher. "The Impact of Music Therapy versus Music Medicine on Psychological Outcomes and Pain in Cancer Patients: A Mixed Methods Study." *Supportive Care in Cancer* 23 (2015): 1261–1271.

Brandes, Vera. "Music as a Medicine: Incorporating Music into Standard Hospital Care." In *Music that Works*, edited by Roland Haas and Vera Brandes. New York: SpringerWienNewYork, 2009.

Brill, Penny, Elaine Abbott, Deborah Benkovitz Williams, Gloria Mou, and Jessi Ryan. *Musicians Handbook*. http://wellness.pittsburghsymphony.org/wp-content/uploads/2016/10/Musicians-Handbook_Accessible-PDF.pdf.

Brooks, Darlene M., Joke Bradt, Lillian Eyre, and Andrea Hunt. "Creative Approaches for Reducing Burnout in Medical Personnel." *The Arts in Psychotherapy* 37, no. 3 (2010): 255–263.

Center for Performing Arts Medicine. *A Guide to Performing as Part of the Margaret Alkek Williams Crain Garden Performance Series*. Houston: Houston Methodist Hospital, 2016. https://www.houstonmethodist.org/~/media/pdf/hr/MusiciansGuideFINAL.ashx?la=en%C2%A0.

Cepeda, M. Soledad, Daniel B. Carr, Joseph Lau, and Hernando Alvarez. "Music for Pain Relief." *Cochrane Database of Systematic Reviews* 2 (2006).

Cleveland Clinic. "Empathy: The Human Connection to Patient Care." YouTube Video. 4:23. February 27, 2013. https://www.youtube.com/watch?v=cDDWvj_q-o8.

"Concert Pianist Inspires Through Music at Hospital, Symphony Gala." *St. Louis Public Radio*. October 17, 2014. https://news.stlpublicradio.org/arts/2014-10-17/concert-pianist-inspires-through-music-at-hospital-symphony-gala.

Davis, Jamal, and Ricky Kendall. "Jamal Davis and Ricky Kendall Cover 'Golden Train' @Shands Hospital." YouTube Video. 3:23. May 19, 2015. https://www.youtube.com/watch?v=72GX-h4a9i8#action=share.

Dileo, Cheryl. *Music Therapy and Medicine: Theoretical and Clinical Applications*. Silver Spring, MD: American Music Therapy Association, 1999.

Dileo, Cheryl, and Joke Bradt. "On creating the Discipline, Profession, and Evidence in the Field of Arts and Healthcare." *Arts & Health* 1, no. 2 (2009): 175.

Drinan, Ann. "The Longwood Symphony: An Interview with Lisa Wong, M.D." Institute for Music Leadership, Eastman School of Music.

Polyphonic Archive. 2012. https://iml.esm.rochester.edu/polyphonic-archive/article/the-longwood-symphony-an-interview-with-lisa-wong-m-d/
Fancourt, Daisy. *Arts in Health: Designing and Researching Interventions.* Oxford: Oxford University Press, 2016. 71.
"Gifts of Art Life Sciences Orchestra." Michigan Medicine. Regents of the University of Michigan. 2013. http://lso.med.umich.edu/about/.
Gioia, Theodore, "Bach at the Burger King." *Los Angeles Review of Books.* May 17, 2018. https://lareviewofbooks.org/article/bach-at-the-burger-king/.
Hirsch, Lily E. *Music in American Crime Prevention and Punishment.* Ann Arbor: University of Michigan Press, 2012.
Kable, Lynn. "Using the Arts to Care for Caregivers." In *Managing Arts Programs in Healthcare*, edited by Patricia Dewey Lambert, 231–243. New York: Routledge, 2016.
Kahn, Andy. "Ron Artis II Performs 'Light the Way' for MyMusicRx Bed-stock 2019." Jambase. July 22, 2019. https://www.jambase.com/article/ron-artis-ii-light-the-way-bedstock-video.
Kendall, Ricky. "Decisions." UF Health Shands Arts in Medicine. University of Florida Health. 2019. https://artsinmedicine.ufhealth.org/2019/08/29/rickys-blog-post-2/.
———. "Interdisciplinary Connection." UF Health Shands Arts in Medicine. University of Florida Health. 2019. https://artsinmedicine.ufhealth.org/2019/08/29/rickys-blog-post-3/.
———. "Jamal." UF Health Shands Arts in Medicine. University of Florida Health. 2019. https://artsinmedicine.ufhealth.org/2019/08/29/rickys-blog-post-4/.
———. "Thankful for Love." SoundCloud audio. Track 1. 2:55. March 27, 2020. https://soundcloud.com/shandsaim/sets/thankful-for-love.
———. "Thankful for Love." SoundCloud audio. 23:11. March 27, 2020. https://soundcloud.com/shandsaim/sets/thankful-for-love.
"Listen." MyMusicRx. Children's Cancer Association. Children's Cancer Association. 2020. https://mymusicrx.org/listen/.
McGroarty, Beth. "Wellness Music." 2020 Wellness Trends. 2020 Global Wellness Summit. 2020. https://www.globalwellnesssummit.com/2020-global-wellness-trends/wellness-music/.
Miller, B.J. 2015. "What Really Matters at the End of Life." Filmed March 2015. TED video. 18:39, https://www.ted.com/talks/bj_miller_what_really_matters_at_the_end_of_life/reading-list?referrer=playlist-505.
"MyMusicRx." Children's Cancer Association. Children's Cancer Association. 2020. https://joyrx.org/programs/mymusicrx/.
O'Callaghan, Clare, and Lucanne Magill, "Effect of Music Therapy on Oncological Staff Bystanders: A Substantive Grounded Theory." *Palliative & Support Care* 7, no. 2 (2009): 219–228.

"Our Programs." Snow City Arts. Snow City Arts. 2016. http://www.snowcityarts.org/what_we_do/ourprogram/.

Pati, Debajyoti. "Positive Distractions." Healthcare Design. Emerald X. March 11, 2010. https://www.healthcaredesignmagazine.com/trends/architecture/positive-distractions/.

The Peabody Institute. *Music for a While Guidelines for Musicians.* Baltimore, MD: Johns Hopkins Peabody Institute. 2020. 4. https://peabody.jhu.edu/wp-content/uploads/2020/10/Music-for-a-While-Guidelines-2020.pdf.

Pories, Susan E., Sorbarikor Piawah, Gregory A. Abel, Sayukta Mullangi, Jennifer Doyle and Joel T. Katz. "What is the Role of the Arts in Medical Education and Patient Care? A Survey-based Qualitative Study." *Journal of Medical Humanities* 39, no. 4 (2018): 431–445.

Preti, Constanza, and Graham F. Welch. "The Inherent Challenges in Creative Musical Performance in a Paediatric Hospital Setting." *Psychology of Music* 41, no. 5 (2012): 647–654.

Reimnitz, Lacey, and Michael J. Silverman. "A randomized Pilot Study of Music Therapy in the Form of Patient-preferred Live Music on Fatigue, Energy and Pain in Hospitalized Adult Oncology Patients on a Blood and Marrow Transplant Unit." *Arts & Health* 12, no. 2 (2020), 154–168.

Roo, Natalie, and Meredith Sheldon. "Tiny Beds, Big Impact." *WUFT News.* April 26, 2018. https://www.wuft.org/news/tiny-beds-big-impact/.

Sen, Yoko. "The Future of Hospital Sound." Healthcare Facilities Symposium and Expo Conference. Austin, TX. September 17, 2019.

Shoemark, Helen, "Sweet Melodies: Combining the Talents and Knowledge of Music Therapy and Elite Musicianship." *Voices: A World Forum for Music Therapy* 9, no. 2 (2009). https://voices.no/index.php/voices/article/view/1819

Slater, Bonny. "Sound Health: The Tranquility Room." GenslerOnCities. Gensler. 2016. http://www.gensleron.com/cities/2018/2/6/sound-health-the-tranquility-room.html

Snow City Arts. "The Ambient Project," released September 8, 2015. Digitally released on Bandcamp. https://snowcityarts.bandcamp.com/album/the-ambient-project.

Sonke, Jill. "Performances in Public Spaces." In *Managing Arts Programs in Healthcare*, edited by Patricia Dewey Lambert, 113–124. New York: Routledge, 2016.

Sonke, Jill, Virginia Pesata, Lauren Arce, Ferol P. Carytsas, Kristen Zemina, and Christine Jokisch. "The Effects of arts-in-medicine programming on the medical-surgical Environment." *Arts & Health: An International Journal for Research, Policy and Practice* 7, no. 1 (2015): 27–41.

State of the Field Committee. *State of the Field Report: Arts in Healthcare 2009.* Washington, DC: Society for the Arts in Healthcare, 2009. 4–5. https://www.americansforthearts.org/sites/default/files/ArtsInHealthcare_0.pdf.

"SymphonyCares at SLU Cancer Center." St. Louis Symphony Orchestra. St. Louis Symphony Orchestra. 2020. https://www.slso.org/en/com/in-the-community/symphonycares/slu-cancer-center/.

Timberg, Scott. "Halt, or I'll play Vivaldi!" *Los Angeles Times*. February 13, 2005. https://www.latimes.com/archives/la-xpm-2005-feb-13-ca-musichurts13-story.html.

"Tiny Bed Sessions with Musicians in Residence." UF Health Shands Arts in Medicine. University of Florida Health. 2020. https://artsinmedicine.ufhealth.org/tiny-bed-sessions/tiny-bed-sessions-with-artists-in-residence/.

Watts, Greg, Amir Khan, and Rob Pheasant. "Influence of Soundscape and Interior Design on Anxiety and Perceived Tranquility of Patients in a Healthcare Setting." *Applied Acoustics* 104 (2016): 135–141.

"What Artbeat Does." Artbeat. Accessed 2020. https://artbeatmusic.org/.

"What is Music Therapy?" American Music Therapy Association. 1998–2020. https://www.musictherapy.org/about/musictherapy/.

Wong, Lisa. *Scales to Scalpels*. New York: Pegasus Books, 2012.

Artist Spotlight 3

Singing from the Soul

Tamara Wellons

I grew up in a small town in rural Virginia next door to my Aunt Corrine. To help my dad, who was her caretaker, I'd walk over to take her a plate and medicine for the day. She'd invite me to her organ and say, "I want to teach you to play this song." I wasn't quick at learning songs on the organ, but I cherish the memories of hearing her alto voice hum and sing many songs. I remember her singing the melody to *The Tennessee Waltz* as she danced in the yard near her pear tree. I'd watch in amazement as she recounted each and every word of the hymns and spirituals she once sang alongside with her sisters—my Grandma Ellen and my Aunt Eunice—as members of the Pritchett Gospel Singers of Newport News. And I'd be astonished when one hour later she would walk over to my dad's house with her slip outside of her dress, unable to remember our earlier conversation and needing to be reminded of who my dad was.

That was my first glimpse at understanding the power of music and how it can trigger memory within a brain that suffered from Alzheimer's. As a teenager, I wasn't able to articulate these experiences in a way that aligned with the science of the brain, but nonetheless, a little seed was planted about the power of music and what it can do for the mind, soul, and body.

For as long as I can remember, I have been a singer. I grew up singing spirituals and hymns at Gilfield Baptist Church in Ivor, Virginia. I mostly sang *a cappella* and in the church choirs. Aside from occasional vocal coaching, I did not formally study music in school. Over the years, I've studied singers to whom I have gravitated—Cynthia Chapman (my hometown church organist and singer), Nancy Wilson, Roberta Flack, and Anita Baker. Interpreting the music of these singers, among others, helped me develop my own sound, performance style, and songwriting skills. My dad, who was taught through oral tradition and modeling, helped me understand how to produce sound and protect my instrument.

But it was years later, after launching a career as a professional singer and refining my own artistic voice, that I began to explore how the many practices learned in my church are useful when singing for others in healthcare settings; how listening, sensing, and being present as learned while studying Reiki, Yoga, and Transcendental Meditation might prepare me to work in the space of arts and healing; and how music might serve as a means for my own health and healing.

I can trace this change of mindset—an understanding of the science behind music's ability to improve health—to an early experience I had while developing a creative music project. I worked with a dancer who told me about the Arts & Humanities Program at Georgetown University's Lombardi Comprehensive Cancer Center. Hearing about her work with patients in hospitals opened my eyes to the possibility of using my voice as a way to help others heal.

After interviewing with the program director, I began my work in this emerging field. I started in the lobby at Lombardi, singing *a cappella* hymns and jazz standards. After quickly gaining the trust of my supervisor, I began to train with her on how to approach patients at their bedside. From the start, connecting with people through my music felt comfortable to me. The more context information I had about the patient, and the more I learned how to observe the physiological changes music was making within the patients' bodies, the more equipped and effective I felt as an artist within this space.

I learned that vulnerability on the part of the artist is essential. And that the details matter. An artist's awareness of the patient's response can make all the difference: the voice can be so penetrating that it can cause discomfort just as easily as it can offer relief. Wrong notes can cause discomfort, too. Understanding vocal control, tone, volume, and sensitivity to sound are critical when working in shifting conditions.

I also learned that singing as a healing art is an intimate act. I remember a patient who thought I was a jukebox. Oh, the excitement that came over her face when she realized that she got to choose what song she wanted to hear! And I cherish each time I could see a little light flicker in her eyes when she'd ask, "Do you know this song?" "Yes." And then off we'd go into a discovery of all of the songs we both know: two people connected through music. Sometimes we'll scroll through song lyrics until a patient asks, "Can you sing this one?" And I say, "Yes, but only if you sing it with me!"

Reflecting on my earliest memories of growing up in Ivor listening to Aunt Corrine sing the spirituals she once sang with the Pritchett Gospel Singers of Newport News, I can now clearly see the sustaining power of music in her life, even as her health deteriorated. In my work in the hospital, I've felt the richness of connecting with people through song, and the comfort of knowing that I have played a part in their well-being. As I imagine my future as performer and healer, I see the healing power of music becoming more integrated into all of my work, regardless of the space I find myself in. And I imagine the wall I have built within myself—separating my perception of commercial success from my recognition of my own worth and unique artistry—coming down as I use my voice in service to others. To heal through sound, regardless of the context, is where I feel validated and called.

3 Training for New Jobs

Professionalizing the Role of the Musician in Healthcare

Jill Sonke

As an artist in residence, I had been working with Maurice "Moe" Ricks, a patient waiting for a heart transplant at University of Florida (UF) Health Shands Hospital, for a few weeks when he was taken into surgery to receive a new heart.

Moe is a recording engineer by trade and was working to piece together a makeshift recording studio in his hospital room. Not wanting to leave that part of his life behind, Moe saw the Arts in Medicine program as an avenue to continue his work and maintain a healthy creative practice within his extended hospitalization. His idea was to record original music in the non-traditional setting of his hospital room. Over the next few weeks, Moe was collecting the necessary equipment and I continued to stop by to play music for him. He was mostly interested in hearing my original music, but he'd frequently have family at his bedside and ask for their requests. Songs would prompt stories from both Moe and his family, giving me a deeper understanding of his life outside the hospital.

I stopped by one day and found Moe's room empty. A nurse pulled me aside and told me that he'd gone to the operating room to receive a heart, but that there had been a complication. The airplane carrying Moe's new heart had struck a flock of birds on takeoff and was forced into an emergency landing far from UF Health. The heart did not survive the trip. Moe, meanwhile, had already undergone the traumatic process of having his chest cavity opened in preparation for the transplant. He woke up after the surgery without a new heart to show for it, and had to be told his own harrowing story by his nurse.

I imagined how disorienting it must be to feel all of the emotion and physical exhaustion associated with a heart transplant only to find that nothing had actually happened. Moe expressed exactly that to me a few days later when I saw him again. While before the surgery, he didn't have a clear idea of what he wanted to record, now Moe wanted to tell his story. And, he was interested in capturing all the perspectives in it. He intuitively recognized that there were others for whom this was a significant ordeal. The doctors on the plane, he figured, must have been afraid for their lives as the cabin of the plane filled with smoke. He asked for my help in turning these stories into a song.[1]

Over the coming days, I collaborated with Moe and our writer in residence to interview several people involved and to put their words to music. We interviewed Moe's nurse, who was the first person he recognized after waking up from surgery—a familiar and comforting face in a moment of uncertainty. We also spoke to the organ procurement doctor who was on the plane and is, in fact, a guitar player himself. In a rare turn of events, I was able to introduce the procurement doctor to the would-be transplant recipient. I sat and played for Moe while the doctor played along on his own guitar. I'm frequently amazed at the power of music to connect people.

It was Moe's intention to use music to ascribe meaning to an event that seemed totally arbitrary, but had affected so many people. When I first played "Waiting" for Moe and his family, he said through tears, "Wow, it's all in there. You guys got everything in there." He went on to express that having his story sung back to him felt like his vision had been realized—almost. The last step was to record it.

In place of a transplanted heart, Moe was given a temporary device that would allow him to return to his life and work at home. Before his discharge from the hospital, we finally got the chance to set up the studio in his room. With cables, microphones, stands, and gear strewn about, Moe sat behind the mixing board and engineered his song. Proud of his story and his new medium with which to tell it, Moe has shared his song with those involved as well as with others as a message of hope and perseverance.

The story you just read provides an example of ways in which a musician in healthcare engages in practice. While the story is written from the perspective of one musician, two UF Health Shands Arts in Medicine musicians in residence, Michael Claytor and Ricky Kendall, worked with the patient throughout his stay in the hospital and engaged in the performance and songwriting activities described.

Musicians like Michael and Ricky engage with people through musical performances and activities in hospitals in support of the holistic goal of enhancing the healthcare experience for patients, family members and visitors, and staff. These interactions reflect the more specialized practices you saw noted in Figure 2.1 in Chapter 2 on the right side of Bentley's taxonomy of types of musical encounters. These musicians possess the skills outlined in Chapter 1, which will be further elaborated on in this chapter. They bring to their work a high level of artistry—as has also been defined in Chapter 1 as the ability to transport, enchant, and affirm dignity amidst extremely challenging circumstances. They are trained to effectively and safely navigate the environment of care, and often function as members of the interprofessional care team.[2]

As you now know, musicians in healthcare may perform for groups of people in public areas of a hospital, such as lobbies and waiting areas, or in clinical care areas, such as inpatient units or infusion suites. They may also provide one-on-one services at patients' bedsides. These one-on-one services will often involve the performance of patient-preferred music, but can also include music making, including shared singing, song-writing, improvisation, composition, sound engineering, or recording, as is described above.

Starting with a brief historical overview of the linkages between music and health, this chapter will further explore the roles of musicians in healthcare and how these musicians are both qualified and prepared to do this work. It will also discuss specific skills and attributes that contribute to effectiveness and success, and that employers expect, among musicians in the field of arts in health. It will also further expand the traditional understanding of musical excellence, to offer a framing that aligns with healthcare satisfaction measures, and extends beyond technical proficiency into the realms of aesthetic experience and self-transcendence. While this book has focused thus far on the voices of musicians, music faculty, and music administrators, this chapter offers the perspective of arts in health administrator and educator, who has hired and supervised musicians in a hospital setting for two decades.

Framing the Work of Musicians in Healthcare

As described in Chapter 2, musicians have worked formally and informally in U.S. healthcare settings since the early 20th century. Their practices follow deep relationships between music and health apparent throughout human history. Evidence of these relationships is found in pre-literate societies and cultures and throughout the evolution of biomedicine.[3] Music-centered healing practices are found across numerous cultures, notably, but not exclusively in Native American, Judaic, Indian, Islamic, Christian, African, Tibetan, Aboriginal, and South American cultures.[4]

One can observe parallels between the disciplines and practitioners of music and medicine considering, for example, Egyptian and Greek history. In early Egypt, the god Thoth was known as the inventor and god of both music and medicine. In Greece, Apollo and Asclepius were gods of both music and of medicine. Parallels such as these pervade human history, with connections between music and health rooted in social, spiritual, cultural, physiologic, and psychologic mechanisms. Plato, Aristotle, and Pythagoras recognized particular qualities of rhythm, tone, and movement that contributed to emotional, spiritual, and physical wellness and healing.[5] In quantifying the relationship between the microcosm and macrocosm by means of mathematics and music, Pythagoras established a direct link between the intervals of the scale and distances between the planets.[6] He, along with other philosophers of the time, proposed that music enables people, at a microcosmic level, to restore essential balance and well-being in accordance with the patterns of harmony in the macrocosm (i.e. the universe). Plato prescribed specific musical rhythms and modes (e.g. Dorian mode) to overcome tension, restoring balance and health. In these ancient practices and in these ways, music was used as an intermediary between body and soul.

Developmental precursors of music and music behaviors across the lifespan and across cultures validate an intense human affinity for music that is closely linked to well-being. These behaviors include forms of play and communication, such as the lyrical ways in which parents communicate and play with infants to enhance the bonding that is essential to a child's survival.[7] In addition, music is central to community practices and rituals that create essential connection and cooperation within groups. Similarly, music is ubiquitously utilized to facilitate presence, transcendence, and connection in religious realms across cultures.[8]

In the 1980s, arts in health began to emerge as a formal discipline in relationship to biomedicine in the United States. A handful of organic, yet intentional, arts programs were developed in hospitals throughout the decade. In 1990, a national organization was developed to support professional advancement of the field (see the current National Organization for Arts in Health (NOAH)). These early programs brought professional artists into healthcare settings to provide performances and opportunities for creative engagements with patients, family members, and caregivers, including aesthetic enhancements and original works of art.

Over the past 40 years, this field has developed and become highly visible. In 2009, the seminal *Arts in Healthcare: State of the Field Report* reported results of field surveys conducted in 2004 and 2007 by the Joint Commission (the national accreditation body for healthcare) that found there were arts programs at approximately half of accredited healthcare institutions in the United States. To day, arts in health is recognized as both a professional field and an academic discipline, and the notion that the arts hold a valuable place in healthcare has become increasingly accepted within the U.S. healthcare system.

Framing Scope of Practice in Healthcare Settings

These enduring traditions of understanding form the foundations of the contemporary practices of both music therapy and music in healthcare. Music therapy, the "clinical and evidence-based use of music interventions to accomplish individualized goals within a therapeutic relationship,"[9] emerged in the 1930s, paving the way for the development of other creative arts therapies such as art therapy, dance movement therapy, and drama therapy. Music therapy coalesced as an academic and professional discipline in the 1950s under the leadership of the National Association for Music Therapy. Music therapists complete academic and supervised clinical training to ensure they are equipped to deploy musical materials and processes safely to customize interventions to achieve mental health or rehabilitation goals. As such, music therapists are clinical care providers who are expert in using music to address clinical goals.

As outlined in the previous chapters, professional musicians who work in healthcare are not clinicians. They work as professional artists who perform, present, or facilitate the arts to enhance the environment of care, provide enjoyment and distraction, and to sometimes assist clinical care partners in achieving *their* clinical goals. These distinctions form the scope of practice for each of these complementary disciplines. A clear understanding of scope of practice is critical to safe, ethical, and impactful music programming and practices in healthcare. Table 3.1 highlights some of the differences in these disciplinary practices, as well as some of the similarities.

Scope of practice in the field of arts in health is guided by a Code of Ethics and Standards of Practice created by the National Organization for Arts in Health.[10] The Code and Standards are available at thenoah.net.

How Musicians Are Prepared to Do this Work

First and foremost, musicians are prepared to do this work through their musical training and experience. We've established the importance of musical excellence, which is built upon artistry as well as

Music in Healthcare and Music Therapy:
A Comparison

	Musician in Healthcare	Music Therapist
Discipline	*Arts in Health*	*Music Therapy*
Practitioner	*Artist/Musician*	*Music Therapist*
Goal	*Enhance healthcare experience*	*Address individualized health goals*
Mechanisms	*Music services/activities* *Performance or creative interaction* *NO psychotherapy or clinical engagement* *NO clinical assessment* *Participation in intervention within a clinician-led partnership*	*Integrated blend of music and counseling* *Bio-psycho-social process* *Psychotherapy or counseling* *Clinical assessment* *Intervention*
Anticipated Outcomes	*Creative opportunities, enjoyment, creative self-expression, meaning-making, connection, distraction*	*Creative opportunities, enjoyment, creative self-expression, meaning-making, distraction, connection, therapeutic process, clinical outcomes*

Table 3.1 (adapted from Sonke et al., 2017) highlights some of the differences in these disciplinary practices, as well as some of the similarities.

mastery of technique and repertoire. As has been discussed, musicians arrive at excellence in a variety of ways, including development that happens within and outside of academic settings. By whatever means a musician achieves a level of artistic proficiency, they must also develop the interpersonal skills required to navigate and work effectively within the healthcare environment. Today, there are an array of opportunities for this education or training, whether within an academic setting or through more practical pathways. These pathways do not typically develop technique or artistry, but rather regard artistry and musical skill as the prerequisites upon which facilitation skills and an understanding of the healthcare context are taught.

There are numerous educational programs for arts in health at accredited universities in the United States. These programs range from undergraduate certificates and minors (most common), to graduate certificates and minors, and graduate degrees.[11] These programs teach scope of practice, ethics, and standards of practice, and generally provide students with hands-on experience in health-care and/or community settings. They range from on-campus to low-residency and fully online delivery formats.

There are also numerous non-academic training and professional development programs available. These programs can be found through web searches or through the National Organization for Arts in Health's website. To discern the quality, depth, and breadth of each program, musicians should compare the curricular offerings of each program with the Standards and Code of Ethics established by the National Organization for Arts in Health.

Currently, there are no standardized minimum qualifications for artists to work in arts in healthcare programs in the United States. There is, however, a current effort underway to establish a national certification for artists in healthcare. This effort is being led by the National Organization for Arts in Health, and is expected to offer a core curriculum for arts in health professionals in 2021, followed by a national certification examination to qualify artists for an *Artists in Healthcare-Certified* (AIH-C) credential. Minimum qualifications will be established for artists to take the certification examination, and it is possible that these qualifications will be generally adopted by the field as minimum qualifications for employment.

Even those with the highest academic credentials in arts in health will need in-depth, on-the-job, regional, and site-specific training and mentorship when working in the healthcare profession. Variations in protocols, procedures, guidelines, and cultures within healthcare institutions demand site-specific orientation. These specialized skills extend to musical preparation, including the development of a broad repertoire that extends across a wide range of musical genres that account for local and regional musical styles and traditions. Consistently delivering meaningful interactions in the healthcare setting hinges on musicians' ability to respond to diverse patient needs. Musical preference has been shown to strongly impact the effectiveness of music in the healthcare setting,[12] making **live preferential music**—music that is selected, based on preference, by the listener and performed live—a standard practice in many arts programs in healthcare settings.

In addition to being prepared to provide individual and group performances in healthcare settings, musicians in healthcare should be prepared to engage patients and others in music making.

As illustrated in Moe's story at the beginning of this chapter, musicians often combine bedside performance and music making in their practices. In the latter capacity, facilitation and songwriting skills are important.

In all of these capacities, we can reflect back to the triad that was discussed earlier in the chapter—presence, artistry, and skill. Together, these aspects of the work of a musician in healthcare provide a basis for **aesthetic experience**, the non-religious experience of transcendence, which is at the heart of it all. More broadly, this triad encapsulates what makes a strong and effective music program in a hospital setting, reminding us that at the core of this work is art. As professionalism advances in the field of arts in health, and while we advance our understanding of the ethics and scope of practice, we must ensure that art remains art. This notion will be explored further in Chapter 4, as we look to a vision for the future of music in healthcare.

What Qualifies a Professional Musician to Work in Healthcare?

While educational standards, professional qualifications, and credentials are yet to be established for the field of arts in health, the

NOAH Standards for Practice: Education

Arts in health professionals:

- Understand professional standards for the role of an artist in health by participating in education related to arts in health;
- Acquire knowledge, techniques, and skills appropriateto their artistic discipline, population, practice setting, role, or situation;
- Demonstrate a commitment to continuing education through self-assessment and professional development; seek opportunities that reflect current practices to develop, maintain, and improve skills and competence in arts in health;
- Maintain professional records that provide evidence of professional experience; and
- Use current research and evidence to increase knowledge of arts in health and enhance professionalism

National Organization for Arts in Health Code of Ethics and Standards for Arts in Health Professionals, 2018, p. 3.

National Organization for Arts in Health's Code of Ethics and Standards define and guide safe and effective practice in the field. The Standards specify that artists are prepared for practice through education or training that provides them with specific abilities that reflect current practice. The Standards are found in the text box "NOAH Standards for Practice: Education."

These standards align with those of other allied health professionals and members of interprofessional care teams in healthcare. All professionals in healthcare environments are expected to demonstrate integrity and compassion, continuously engage in professional development, and communicate and collaborate effectively with other health professionals. Musicians engaged with arts in health are not exempt from these expectations. NOAH standards emphasize not only music skills (as discussed in Chapter 1), but also **professionalism**—the ability to make decisions, behave, and interact in ways expected of all those working in healthcare environments. Professionalism and musicianship enable arts in health practitioners to work as highly valued members of the interdisciplinary care team in healthcare settings.

The story at the beginning of this chapter illustrates both musical skill and professionalism in action. Michael notes that he "imagined how disorienting it must be to feel all of the emotion and physical exhaustion associated with a heart transplant only to find that nothing had actually happened." He brings this compassion and empathy to his direct interactions with Moe, as well as to the artistic decisions he makes in working with Moe. We also see in this story Michael's ability to collaborate with other members of the healthcare team, which was essential to bringing Moe's vision to fruition. Yet, while music can be a tremendous asset in the healthcare environment when it is offered in this way, we must also consider its potential to be a liability as well.

First and Foremost, Do No Harm

While much research supports the ways in which many people routinely use music to enhance mood states,[13] studies of music in the healthcare environment suggest that, while it is also quite efficacious, particular care must be taken in regard to the delivery of music in this setting.[14] As was described in Impromptu 1, "Music and Health and the Health of Music," with even the finest musical performance, "the space is even more hectic and louder than before J.S. Bach began." Music—like any added element—*contributes to the complexity of the healthcare environment.* If brought with awareness and conscious intention, it can bring profound benefits; but if it lacks this awareness, it can cause negative distraction, stress, and can even compromise immune function and patient safety.[15] And, music, like any other element in healthcare, must—first and foremost—**do no harm.**

The potential for harm may be difficult for those who love music to fully understand; it certainly was for the pioneers of the arts in health field. Recognizing the power and potential of music, some early programs sought to bring as much music as possible into healthcare settings. However, the evolution and examination of practice and formal research soon helped program leaders and musicians to recognize that music must be provided at the right time, in the right place, and in the right way in order for it to be safe and helpful.[16] In addition to developing the presence and "*being*" described by Fernández Via in Impromptu 2, the perceived high quality, or excellence, of the music is one of the factors that mitigates the potential negative impacts of music in the complex healthcare environment. But, we know these sorts of judgments are highly subjective and difficult to define. So how do we, as employers of musicians in healthcare, define and maintain quality standards for music in healthcare? How do we create standards for something that is so subjective and elusive? How do we decide who and what is good enough? Let's start with healthcare's patient satisfaction paradigm.

In healthcare, patient satisfaction is a primary concern and objective. Satisfaction is often considered in relation to dissatisfiers (basic needs not fulfilled), satisfiers (specific characteristics or expectations met), and delighters (unexpected elements that exceed expectations). In business, dissatisfaction closes a business, satisfaction keeps it afloat, and delight drives its growth. In healthcare, the differences across this spectrum have more critical implications for patient safety and outcomes.

By All Means, Delight Them

In assessing something as subjective as musical excellence, the concept of the "**delighter**" is useful and can be applied to selection of musicians whose level of artistry and technical proficiency will be most suitable to the healthcare environment. It is important to remember here that, as described in Chapter 1, the most important "ingredients" of excellence in the context of arts in health are the ability to transport, enchant, and affirm. There are no objective criteria. Rather, the likelihood of consistent positive subjective experiences to result from the musician's artistry must be assessed.

In arts in health programs, auditions are a standard component of the hiring process. Audition panels are ideally made up of individuals who represent the hospital's administrative and clinical purviews, along with those with experience and expertise in music and in management and practice in arts in healthcare programming. These individuals will collectively and collaboratively assess aspects of the performance, such as technical mastery (broadly framed from the standpoint of any musical tradition), breadth of repertoire, presence, and interpersonal connection. And, the concept of delight is important here in regard to the holistic assessment the panelists will offer.

In an audition for a position within the healthcare setting, a performance that delights the audition panel likely exceeds the panelists expectations by being more emotionally engaging and technically proficient, and by providing an aesthetic experience that enchants and transports. Even across diverse preferences and standards, and across diverse repertoire and musical traditions, quality can be assessed in relation to how something measures up to previous auditions and musicians, hired and not hired. So, when a musical performance registers as outstanding as compared to other or most performances, the panel can assume that responses of those served by the musician will likely be positive, even when taking into account the diverse populations and traditions of the patients the healthcare system serves.

As artists, we can take this concept of delight a few steps further as well, to explore the notions of flow and self-transcendence. Historically, human beings have engaged in aesthetic experience through the arts as a means for experiencing both ecstasy and self-transcendence. Ecstasy was the driving force in the Dionysian dance rituals of the ancient Greeks and at the 1969 Woodstock music festival. It takes delight to the next level, to *rapturous* delight, wherein one is transported from a normal state of being into a state of heightened feeling.

Throughout human history, music has been, and continues to be, among the most recognized and embraced means for achieving this transcendence. It is used as a daily salve for balancing body, mind, and spirit, as well as a routine means for quieting and expanding the mind in spiritual practices across cultures. And, in this transported state, we are more apt to experience **self-transcendence**, or expand our conceptual boundaries—the ways in which we see ourselves or the world around us.[17] The hymn, *Amazing Grace*, captures this experience in the line "I was blind, but now I see," referring to insight that alters one's conceptual boundaries, or previous world views. In a healthcare context, self-transcendence has been linked to enhanced wellbeing, or sense of wholeness, among both patients and staff.[18] Pamela Reed, in her "Demystifying self-transcendence for mental health nursing practice and research," found that in moments of vulnerability (such as when we experience illness and hospitalization), people are particularly susceptible to self-transcendence, and that the arts can be a means for facilitating self-transcendence.[19]

The connections among vulnerability, self-transcendence, and wellbeing are powerful ones, and should be recognized, in relation to the role of a musician in healthcare and the skills that must be possessed. In this role, a musician does not use music prescriptively or curatively. Or, as we read in Impromptu 2, "Fixing, Doing, Being," the musician does not need to "fix" anything. This would involve making clinical decisions that a musician is not qualified to make in regard to what a patient may need. Rather, the musician recognizes the power of music, and in responding to a patient will make artistic decisions that are informed by an understanding of the healthcare context and any specific information that clinical partners or the patient may provide. As the musician develops a higher level of skill, she will also be able to maintain that presence and responsiveness within a **flow state**, in which she is completely immersed or absorbed in the activity of playing, and may experience a merging of action and awareness. In this flow state, the musician can unleash her full artistry, while years of practice and technical skill are brought effortlessly to bear.[20]

Music performed with a high level of perceived artistry and excellence may be more likely to allow the listener to be transported. In the healthcare setting, this transportation can provide a distraction from pain, anxiety, and preoccupation with illness. The value of this kind of distraction cannot be overstated, as it can have profoundly positive effects, physically and emotionally. Conversely, a lack of excellence could result in preoccupation with technique or simply in an uninterested disregard for the performance. And, it is also important to recognize that, while music has been widely shown to reduce stress, it has also been shown to increase stress and decrease immune response—the exact opposite of its intention. For example, a study of the effects of choral singing and listening found improvements in emotional affect and immune function among the singers, while the listeners had an increase in negative affect and decreases in immune function.[21] These findings, reflected in Artist Spotlight 3 with Tamara Wellons' understanding that "wrong notes can cause discomfort," underscore the importance of both preference and artistic excellence, and also point to the need for an artist in healthcare to develop keen observation and perception skills.

How Employers View and Value Skills and Attributes

Musical excellence is just one factor of quality in relation to hospital-based music. In healthcare settings, quality is also assessed in relation to the appropriateness of the music within the setting, to the people involved, and to the moment. In order to achieve this type of quality, a musician must be able to constantly notice (through observation) and decode (through perception) clues related to the needs of the people in the space. This is a complex task, and requires a specific array of skills and attributes, such as observation, perception, responsiveness, adaptability, empathy, self-awareness, presence, and clarity. It is important to note, that what we refer to here as attributes can be learned, practiced, and developed. For the purposes of this discussion, we'll think of attributes as the characteristics or qualities that a musician might naturally exhibit in coming to this work, and skills are competencies that are learned. It is important to note here that attributes, such as self-awareness, humility, and compassion, may also be learned and, as such, become a part of the skillset of a musician in healthcare. We differentiate them here to note that some of a person's natural qualities and tendencies can be assets in relation to building the relational skills necessary to work effectively as a musician in healthcare.

In the telling of Moe's story, Michael illustrates these skills and attributes. In the story, Michael said that he imagined what Moe might be feeling after his surgery. From that empathetic perspective, he listened to Moe's interests and responded by offering to help him craft a song. This interaction, and the artistic choices Michael made as a facilitator within the song-writing process were informed by all that Michael had observed and heard from Moe and his family while performing for them during his earlier visits. We also see in the story that Michael continuously tracked his own experience, as well as Moe's, within their interactions. In a situation of this intensity, as is common in a hospital, self-awareness and personal boundaries are essential. Musicians must self-reflect in order to gauge their capacity to remain present and responsive with a patient and to make choices that are in the best interest of not only the patient, but also their own personal boundaries.

Sustaining the Work through Personal Boundaries and Self-Care

It is easy in a healthcare setting, where needs are compelling, to ignore and override one's own boundaries. For example, playing music for a patient who is finding much needed relaxation in the midst of a stressful hospital stay is extremely fulfilling and can, in the moment, feel much more important than taking a lunch break or getting to another commitment on time. But, going beyond the boundaries of a scheduled shift can create physical or practical repercussions that, if habituated, will make the work unsustainable. Similarly, if an artist is unable to recognize when exposure to certain situations is beyond their own emotional capacity or comfort, secondary trauma can occur, which will quickly lead to compassion fatigue and burnout. So, keeping good personal boundaries is a critical skill for enabling musicians in residence to provide safe and meaningful services, and also for enabling longevity in the role.[22] Let's look at another example from Michael's practice.

> *I met the family through a referral from a nurse on the unit. The patient was unresponsive and the family had asked the nurse to call us [Arts in Medicine] so that they could all hear some music together as a family before withdrawing care that afternoon. It was a very heavy room—there were four family members at the bedside, each interacting with their loved one and coping in different ways. His daughter welcomed me in warmly, and told me about his music taste. He loved Bob Dylan, and his wife jumped in to suggest that I play "Blowin' in the Wind." In these situations, it's clear to me that I'm an accessory to this family having a very difficult but very meaningful moment. Knowing that, I try really hard to read the room and play to the mood as much as possible. I ask only the most essential questions of them, so that they can fully focus on their moment with their loved one. This visit was a good example of that. As I played, the family wasn't paying attention to me so much as they were using the music I was playing as a way to connect with patient. They asked for a second song, and someone suggested George Harrison. I played "Here Comes the Sun," and the patient's loved ones laid their hands on him, smiling difficult smiles. I could tell after two songs that my job was done, so I thanked them for inviting me in and stepped out. I was trying very hard to keep my presence light and neutral—neither overly sympathetic nor upbeat, so it was only after leaving that the impact of the moment hit me.*

In this interaction, Michael demonstrated an array of skills and attributes that make him an effective practitioner and also enable him to sustain the work in a meaningful way. He placed himself as an "accessory" to the family, rather than as a performer who expects or needs an audience's attention. He used his observational skills to "read the room," so that he could bring an appropriate and unobtrusive energy to a very delicate and sacred situation—"neither overly sympathetic or overly upbeat." He asks as few questions as possible as he obtains musical preference from the family, and knows when to leave. Some might describe this synthesis of skills and attributes as intuition, which can be perceived as a strong and clear feeling about something. But, Michael's decisions come from much more than feeling. They are informed by presence, humility, and observation in the present moment, and by his experience and clear understanding of the intent and scope of his practice and the healthcare environment.

This scenario also demonstrates the profound meaningfulness of this work. What could be more meaningful than bringing beauty and making an experience of loss a little more bearable for a family? It also demonstrates the intensity of the work, and the need for boundaries and self-care to manage the "impact of the moment." Working as a musician in healthcare can be exceedingly meaningful, but requires clear boundaries and good self-care. Good self-care means taking all the routinized steps necessary to be truly present in a challenging environment and in an other-oriented, or helping role. For most people, this means getting good rest, eating well, exercising, playing, socializing, or developing other self-care practices. It also means being adept at self-reflecting and knowing just how much you can give in a particular moment. It means understanding the symptoms of **compassion fatigue** and burnout, and having a support system in place if the musician experiences exhaustion from caring for others.

Functioning as a Member of the Interprofessional Care Team

Healthcare is a unique culture, and is quite different than arts culture. To be successful working in a hospital and as a member of the **interprofessional care team** (a group of professionals from varied disciplines who collaborate in a team-based approach to provide integrated care), an artist must be able to adapt to healthcare culture, which includes understanding, respecting, and complying with many detailed and constantly changing policies and procedures.

In this way, skills and attributes translate to on-the-job behaviors. A high level of adherence to policies and procedures is critical to an artist's success and effectiveness in the healthcare environment.

In our program's three decades of hiring musicians at UF Health Shands, our hardest lessons have come when we have failed to openly discuss and critically asses an artist's ability to respect and adapt to healthcare culture. Part of this assessment comes through imposing administrative steps that require a candidate to demonstrate their ability to adapt to the expectations of healthcare culture, including timely completion of mandated hospital training programs, and daily and weekly documentation and reporting. We also carefully assess the artist's effective participation in communication and practice protocols on clinical units, and institute trial periods supported by highly structured mentorship and supervision.

Adherence to healthcare standards and practices not only ensures patient safety, but also places the musician on par with other primary and allied health care providers in regard to professionalism. This professionalism and participation in healthcare culture means that an artist can function as a member of the interprofessional care team and help contribute to the provision of the highest level of whole person care. When musicians function as members of this interprofessional care team, healthcare providers can understand their practices and can feel confident in making the referrals that enable music services to be provided to patients. These relationships and referral systems are essential to programing music in healthcare. In Chapter 4, you'll learn more about partnership skills, which are at the heart of functioning as a part of this interprofessional care team.

Notes

1 See "When tragedy strikes: UF Health's Transplant team risks their lives for Moe Ricks" video and download an mp3 of Moe's song at https://m.ufhealth.org/birdstrike.

2 Jill Sonke, Virginia Pesata, Jenny Baxley Lee and John Graham-Pole, "Nurse perceptions of artists as collaborators in interprofessional care teams," *Healthcare* 5, no. 3 (2017): 50.

3 Daisy Fancourt, Aaron Williamon, Livia A Carvalho, Andrew Steptoe, Rosie Dow, and Ian Lewis, "Singing modulates mood, stress, cortisol, cytokine and neuropeptide activity in cancer patients and carers," *Ecancermedicalscience* 10 (2016). See also Michael H Thaut, "Music as therapy in early history," *Progress in Brain Research* 217 (2015): 143–158.

4 Gregory Ghent, *African alchemy: Art for healing in African societies* (Moraga: Hearst Art Gallery, Saint Mary's College of California, 1994). Peregrine Horden, ed., *Music as medicine: The history of music*

therapy since antiquity (New York: Routledge, 2017). Ake Hultkrantz, *Shamanic healing and ritual drama: Health and medicine in Native North American religious traditions* (Spring Valley: Crossroad, 1992).

5 Claudius Conrad, "Music for healing: From magic to medicine," *The Lancet* 376, no. 9757 (2010): 1980–1981. Sonja Weiss, "Medicine for body or soul? Philosophical reconstruction of the role of music in ancient healing practices," *Muzikoloski Zbornik* 52, no. 1 (2016): 171.

6 Christopher Callahan, "Music in Medieval medical practice: Speculations and certainties," *College Music Symposium* 40 (2000): 151–164.

7 Ellen Dissanayake, "If music is the food of love, what about survival and reproductive success?" *Musicae Scientiae* 12, no. 1_suppl (2008): 169–195.

8 Ferdia J Stone-Davis, *Music and transcendence* (New York: Routledge, 2015).

9 "Definition and Quotes about Music Therapy," American Music Therapy Association, American Music Therapy Association, 1998–2020, https://www.musictherapy.org/about/musictherapy/.

10 "Code of Ethics for Arts in Health Professionals and Standards for Arts in Health Professionals," The National Organization for Arts in Health, National Organization for Arts in Health, 2018, https://thenoah.net/wp-content/uploads/2019/01/NOAH-Code-of-Ethics-and-Standards-for-Arts-in-Health-Professionals.pdf.

11 Jill Sonke, Jenny B Lee, Max Helgemo, Judy Rollins, Ferol Carytsas, Susan Imus, Patricia Dewey Lambert, "Arts in health: Considering language from an educational perspective in the United States," *Arts & Health* 10, no. 2 (2018): 151–164.

12 Soledad M Cepeda, Daniel B Carr, Joseph Lau, and Hernando Alvarez, "Music for pain relief," *Cochrane Database of Systematic Reviews* 2 (2006). Cheryl Dileo, *Music therapy and medicine: Theoretical and clinical applications* (Silver Spring: American Music Therapy Association, 1999). Lacey Reimnitz and Michael J Silverman, "A randomized pilot study of music therapy in the form of patient-preferred live music on fatigue, energy and pain in hospitalized adult oncology patients on a blood and marrow transplant unit," *Arts & Health* 12, no. 2 (2020): 154–168. Wolfgang Schmid and David Aldridge, "Active music therapy in the treatment of multiple sclerosis patients: A matched control study," *Journal of Music Therapy* 41, no. 3 (2004): 225–240. Michael J Silverman, Lorissa Letwin, and Louisa Nuehring, "Patient preferred live music with adult medical patients: A systematic review to determine implications for clinical practice and future research," *The Arts in Psychotherapy* 49 (2016): 1–7.

13 Fancourt et al., "Singing modulates mood." Saoirse Finn and Daisy Fancourt, "The biological impact of listening to music in clinical and nonclinical settings: A systematic review," *Progress in Brain Research* 237 (2018): 173–200. Cori L Pelletier, "The effect of music on decreasing arousal due to stress: A meta-analysis," *Journal of Music Therapy* 41, no. 3 (2004): 192–214.

14 Cheryl Dileo, "Effects of music and music therapy on medical patients: A meta-analysis of the research and implications for the future," *Journal of the Society for Integrative Oncology* 4, no. 2 (2006): 67–70. Joanna

Briggs Institute, "The Joanna Briggs Institute best practice information sheet: Music as an intervention in hospitals," *Nursing & Health Sciences* 13, no. 1 (2011): 99–102. Jill Sonke, "Professionalizing the arts in healthcare field," in *Managing arts programs in healthcare*, ed. Patricia Dewey Lambert (New York: Routledge, 2015), 50–62.

15 Thomas G Kannampallil, Guido F Schauer, Trevor Cohen, and Vimla L Patel, "Considering complexity in healthcare systems," *Journal of Biomedical Informatics* 44, no. 6 (2011): 943–947. See also Jill Sonke, Virginia Pesata, Lauren Arce, Ferol P Carytsas, Kristen Zemina, and Christine Jokisch, "The effects of arts-in-medicine programming on the medical-surgical work environment," *Arts & Health* 7, no. 1 (2015): 27–41.

16 Sonke, "Arts in health," 151–164. See also Jill Sonke, "The effects of arts-in-medicine programming," 27–41.

17 Viktor E Frankl, "Self-transcendence as a human phenomenon," *Journal of Humanistic Psychology* 6, no. 2 (1966): 97–106. Pamela G Reed, "Pamela Reed's theory of self-transcendence," *Nursing Theories Nursing Practice* (2010): 417.

18 Doris D Coward and Pamela G Reed, "Self-transcendence: A resource for healing at the end of life," *Issues in Mental Health Nursing* 17, no. 3 (1996): 275–288. Beth Palmer, Mary T Quinn Griffin, Pamela Reed, and Joyce J Fitzpatrick, "Self-transcendence and work engagement in acute care staff registered nurses," *Critical Care Nursing Quarterly* 33, no. 2 (2010): 138–147. Pamela G Reed, "Demystifying self-transcendence for mental health nursing practice and research," *Archives of Psychiatric Nursing* 23, no. 5 (2009): 397–400.

19 Reed, "Demystifying self-transcendence," 397–398.

20 Mihaly Csikszentmihalyi, Sami Abuhamdeh, and Jeanne Nakamura, "Flow," in *Flow and the foundations of positive psychology* (Berlin: Springer, 2014), 227–238.

21 Gunter Kreutz, Stephan Bongard, Sonja Rohrmann, Volker Hodapp, and Dorothee Grebe, "Effects of choir singing or listening on secretory immunoglobulin A, cortisol, and emotional state," *Journal of Behavioral Medicine* 27, no. 6 (2004): 623–635.

22 Costanza Preti and Graham F Welch, "The inherent challenges in creative musical performance in a paediatric hospital setting," *Psychology of Music* 41, no. 5 (2013): 647–664.

Bibliography

Callahan, Christopher. "Music in medieval medical practice: Speculations and certainties." *College Music Symposium* 40 (2000): 151–164.

Cepeda, M Soledad, Daniel B Carr, Joseph Lau, and Hernando Alvarez. "Music for pain relief." *Cochrane Database of Systematic Reviews* 2 (2006): 1–56.

"Code of Ethics for Arts in Health Professionals and Standards for Arts in Health Professionals." The National Organization for Arts in Health. The National Organization for Arts in Health. 2018. https://thenoah.net/wp-content/uploads/2019/01/NOAH-Code-of-Ethics-and-Standards-for-Arts-in-Health-Professionals.pdf.

Conrad, Claudius. "Music for healing: From magic to medicine." *The Lancet* 376, no. 9757 (2010): 1980–1981.

Coward, Doris D, and Pamela G Reed."Self-transcendence: A resource for healing at the end of life." *Issues in Mental Health Nursing* 17, no. 3 (1996): 275–288.

Csikszentmihalyi, Mihaly, Sami Abuhamdeh, and Jeanne Nakamura. "Flow." In *Flow and the foundations of positive psychology*, edited by Mihaly Csikszentmihalyi, 227–238. Berlin: Springer, 2014.

"Definitions and Quotes about Music Therapy." American Music Therapy Association. 2018. https://www.musictherapy.org/about/quotes/.

Dileo, Cheryl. "Effects of music and music therapy on medical patients: A meta-analysis of the research and implications for the future." *Journal of the Society for Integrative Oncology* 4, no. 2 (2006): 67–70.

———. *Music therapy and medicine: Theoretical and clinical applications.* Silver Spring: American Music Therapy Association, 1999.

Dissanayake, Ellen. "If music is the food of love, what about survival and reproductive success?" *Musicae Scientiae* 12, no. 1_suppl (2008): 169–195.

Fancourt, Daisy, Aaron Williamon, Livia A Carvalho, Andrew Steptoe, Rosie Dow, and Ian Lewis. "Singing modulates mood, stress, cortisol, cytokine and neuropeptide activity in cancer patients and carers." *Ecancermedicalscience* 10 (2016): 1–13.

Finn, Saoirse and Daisy Fancourt. "The biological impact of listening to music in clinical and nonclinical settings: A systematic review." *Progress in Brain Research* 237 (2018): 173–200.

Frankl, Viktor E. "Self-transcendence as a human phenomenon." *Journal of Humanistic Psychology* 6, no. 2 (1966): 97–106.

Ghent, Gregory. *African alchemy: Art for healing in african societies.* Moraga: Hearst Art Gallery, Saint Mary's College of California, 1994.

Horden, Peregrine, ed. *Music as medicine: The history of music therapy since antiquity.* New York: Routledge, 2017.

Hultkrantz, Åke. *Shamanic healing and ritual drama: Health and medicine in native north american religious traditions.* Spring Valley: Crossroad, 1992.

Joanna Briggs Institute. "The Joanna Briggs Institute best practice information sheet: Music as an intervention in hospitals." *Nursing & Health Sciences* 13, no. 1 (2011): 99–102.

Kreutz, Gunter, Stephan Bongard, Sonja Rohrmann, Volker Hodapp, and Dorothee Grebe. "Effects of choir singing or listening on secretory immunoglobulin A, cortisol, and emotional state." *Journal of Behavioral Medicine* 27, no. 6 (2004): 623–635.

Palmer, Beth, Mary T Quinn Griffin, Pamela Reed, and Joyce J Fitzpatrick. "Self-transcendence and work engagement in acute care staff registered nurses." *Critical Care Nursing Quarterly* 33, no. 2 (2010): 138–147.

Pelletier, Cori L. "The effect of music on decreasing arousal due to stress: A Meta-analysis." *Journal of Music Therapy* 41, no. 3 (2004): 192–214.

Reed, Pamela G. "Demystifying self-transcendence for mental health nursing practice and research." *Archives of Psychiatric Nursing* 23, no. 5 (2009): 397–400.

———. "Pamela Reed's theory of self-transcendence." *Nursing Theories and Nursing Practice* (2010): 417–427.

Reimnitz, Lacey, and Michael J Silverman. "A randomized pilot study of music therapy in the form of patient-preferred live music on fatigue, energy and pain in hospitalized adult oncology patients on a blood and marrow transplant unit." *Arts & Health* 12, no. 2 (2020): 154–168.

Schmid, Wolfgang, and David Aldridge. "Active music therapy in the treatment of multiple sclerosis patients: A matched control study." *Journal of Music Therapy* 41, no. 3 (2004): 225–240.

Silverman, Michael J, Lorissa Letwin, and Louisa Nuehring. "Patient preferred live music with adult medical patients: A systematic review to determine implications for clinical practice and future research." *The Arts in Psychotherapy* 49 (2016): 1–7.

Sonke, Jill. "Professionalizing the arts in healthcare field." In *Managing arts programs in healthcare*, edited by Patricia Dewey Lambert, 50–62. New York: Routledge, 2015.

Sonke, Jill, Jenny B Lee, Max Helgemo, Judy Rollins, Ferol Carytsas, Susan Imus, Patricia Dewey Lambert. "Arts in health: Considering language from an educational perspective in the United States." *Arts & Health* 10, no. 2 (2018): 151–164.

Sonke, Jill, Virginia Pesata, Lauren Arce, Ferol P Carytsas, Kristen Zemina, and Christine Jokisch. "The effects of arts-in-medicine programming on the medical-surgical work environment." *Arts & Health* 7, no. 1 (2015): 27–41.

Sonke, Jill, Virginia Pesata, Jenny Baxley Lee, and John Graham-Pole. "Nurse perceptions of artists as collaborators in interprofessional care teams." *Healthcare*, vol. 5, no. 3, p. 50. Multidisciplinary Digital Publishing Institute, 2017.

State of the Field Committee. *State of the field report: Arts in healthcare 2009*. Washington, DC: Society for the Arts in Healthcare, 2009.

Stone-Davis, Ferdia J. *Music and transcendence*. New York: Routledge, 2016.

Thaut, Michael H. "Music as therapy in early history." *Progress in Brain Research* 217 (2015): 143–158.

Weiss, Sonja. "Medicine for body or soul? Philosophical reconstruction of the role of music in ancient healing practices." *Muzikoloski Zbornik* 52, no. 1 (2016): 171.

Moisès Fernández Via: *Fixing*, calligraphy, ink on paper, 2019.

Impromptu 2
Fixing, Doing, Being

Moisès Fernández Via

Continuity is to blame. It extends good and bad unapologetically. Our first sip of tea is a revolution; pure power. But soon after, we feel cheated, as if the tea had been steeped in some sort of liquid boredom. It is not an issue of time per se—it is not that sipping tea at Noon is epic, and then the whole thing goes down the drain one minute past. It is also not a matter of fickleness—we could remain completely petrified and immovable for hours, but we will not succeed at turning off an experience of beginning, middle, and end coming out of that silly stillness. Even all the clocks on earth could be destroyed provoking a cosmic jetlag, yet continuity will continue, untouched.

Continuity is a rather technical term to say life. It is the same old thing but continuously same, continuously old, and hence happening. A sense of experience is taking place all the time.

Pain knows about that more than anything else; it fights continuity and needs it at the same time. That's why it's painful. Pain needs continuity to ease, yet continuity is what brings it back. In other words, illness relies on health to ease, even when health is what temporarily holds illness. Now you understand why continuity is to blame.

Continuity seems to be life's basic language. There is no eventfulness possible outside of that. Sipping a cup of tea, quitting your job, falling in love, or dying are distinctively colored ways to go about continuity. I am not saying they all have the same taste or texture. Their implications are clearly rich and diverse. But despite their differences, they cannot help but to wear life's finest garment over and over: an original spark that extends its qualities and resonance longing for a decisive moment to merge with in ease.

We could call that experience, perception, or truth. It is not a matter of words. But the main point is to make sure our idea of health is plugged to that power—to the basic experience of life as it is. Seeing, hearing, smelling, tasting, touching, and feeling *that* very continuity is health.

Healing

Let me share with you a story. One day, I was seated in a corner of a lobby at Boston Medical Center. Nothing special was going on, just the ordinary hecticness of people moving across the lobby. But suddenly, from afar, I saw an old Black woman walking very slowly. One step. Then another one. If it wasn't for a gorgeous pink fabric skillfully wrapped around her head, and a cart heavy as an anchor full of life, I am sure she would have disappeared from everyone's eyes—a lost Nubian queen moving in an invisible sad-elegant slowness through space.

It touched me. Every step of her journey moved me deeply. She arrived where I was. She stopped, looked at me, and said: "*p-i-a-n-o*." Each one of the twenty years I spent training as a pianist rejoiced. Music was needed and I was there.

I had never seen that woman before. Nor can I understand how she knew I was a pianist. But I swear I would have moved to that upright piano in the middle of the lobby and played for her regardless—even if I wouldn't have had a clue about how to do it.

The situation was so real and charged that I became unable to go to the Frédéric Chopin concerto I find myself so often playing. Instead, my right hand started to move slowly at a cloud-like pace. A gentle, dignified impromptu cadenza was making her way through space. My left hand supported that with profound chords, like a heavy anchor sinking deep down the keyboard. Standing in front of the piano, the Nubian queen cried the whole time. When the music concluded she made a simple gesture in appreciation and left. I have never seen that woman again.

Was that situation therapy? I must say no. It had no agenda. It was a genuine encounter based on unrehearsed appreciation—seeing and being seen at once for who we are. Keys were being pressed down and tears followed that same direction. It doesn't matter who did what, but it happened. The only case history, the only diagnosis at hand, was to honor how the situation was unfolding. That was enough. Playing was not trying to fix anything in any of us. On the contrary, it brought more of her and me to the surface at that very moment. And to our surprise, the spontaneous fruition was a piano making tangible the beauty of that undoubtful strength that carried a gorgeous pink fabric skillfully wrapped around her head, and a cart heavy as an anchor full of life.

In Italian *piano* also means softly, slowly. *Piano si va lontano*—step by step one reaches far. The why of that situation will remain unknown, but its sharp clarity speaks undeniably loudly: She said *piano*; she asked exactly for the gentle slow quality that she already was and encountering that brought her to tears. Ladies and gentlemen, that is the image of healing.

Whoever you are Nubian queen, wherever you might be now: I honor you and thank you fondly, for you taught the power of *being* and that healing—like piano playing or any other *doing*—can effortlessly blossom from that ground.

In my modest opinion, the whole of music and health—creativity and wellbeing for that matter—is contained in that story. To put it in one sentence: **in the context of care, music communicates sanity.**

Music gets our pain. It gets the heavy claustrophobia we drag across time for constantly needing and rejecting continuity; for being so allergic to our own experience. To the intelligence of our senses, music uncovers a resolved form to hold each moment; a lighter open way to be in space. It does not preach about it, but it actually allows us to feel that possibility directly.

Engaging through the senses with music becomes to stage in our own bodies how dissonance and consonance can be equally held, and together, be brought to their next thing free of struggle. It rescues a fresh and unspoiled relationship to continuity that is always accessible.

There is an extended myth about music bringing us to places, but the truth is that music brings us back to the workable side of right this, right here, and right now. Name any emotion and feeling ever possible and bring it into its sound equivalent. To your surprise, you will discover the way in which it naturally shifts without the barricades of moralistic traps. Music—that fleeing thing void of any solid substance—seems to master the art of being human. Music is a total absence of being lazy to be human, and that is its power and health. (Continuity is to blame, again.)

Burnout

At this point, wearing white coats and playing doctors as musicians would feel like a deceptive carnival. Why take that shortcut? Music is not about fixing; it is not even about the momentary boost after choosing *these* versus *that*. It is about igniting a wholesome culture of *being* on the spot—a totality skillfully embraced. Fixing creates burnout. It's like a short-cut leading to an unexpected cul-de-sac.

Something reveals complexity and richness, and in absolute panic we bang it down with our handy hammer—done; next thing. You see? Even fixing is about bringing a moment to its next one. But it manufactures it, neurotically. Fixing looks for a quick feeling of power over any undomesticated complexity. But in doing so, it exercises the forgetfulness of our basic confidence to just *be*. The main issue is that it overworks, it over-does everything, and burns out. It labors unnecessarily doubting a capability and a strength that are already available. It is so much work.

If we let that attitude run our businesses, it will turn anything (healthcare—or conservatories, for the same matter) into large buildings with expensive equipment, full of overworked, unhappy individuals. A *fixing* culture will provide plenty of tricks and gadgets to entertain our couldn't-care-less, but it will make everyone feel like a nuisance. And that hurts.

In a way, we are all sick of this self-imposed diaspora from our strength and worthiness. Fixing sets us further and further away from that. It keeps us always on the run, never able to fully take our seat of undoubtful dignity.

Being is the alternative—a soothing unconditional ground. Worthiness is ever-present there, and whatever action we engage with is precisely how we celebrate that. On the contrary, fixing is an unnecessary inflammation.

That is the flip I propose: an avant-garde of a healing culture envisioned and executed with a profound appreciation of what it means to be human. Quite frankly, the solution cannot be swallowing more pills, more numbness, and further laziness to full human-beingness. At the right point, we just need to finally engage with our situation and experience our worthiness back.

That applies to music as much as it applies to hospitals. Conservatories don't need to cure people from their inability to play music "well." They just need to be a rich environment where individuals are guided to reclaim their own wisdom. "Playing well" is not a foreign experience that needs to be forcefully imposed at all costs, but a direct consequence of nurturing genuine worthiness and strength.

I just said "playing well" but we could say "health" instead: Health is not a foreign experience that needs to be forcefully imposed at all costs, but a direct consequence of nurturing genuine worthiness and strength. Such view goes as far as to recognize the imbalance of illness as an expression of basic health.

A whole system could be engineered as an opportunity for individuals to be reminded of their worthiness and strength. I would add unconditionally.

Healthcare could look, sound, and feel like the space in which the intelligence, the skill, and the sacredness of care manifest. Care is not a war, and although it demands the knowledge of science, it ultimately is the wisdom of an art. **Care is compassion in action**. And whatever energy is left after that demanding practice, we should put it to tirelessly say "No" to whatever doubts worthiness.

The flip is not "fixing the fixing" but doing even the wrong thing in the most beautiful way. That unplugs the whole fixing inflammation. It might seem crazy, but if we let the wisdom of music, art, and creativity run healthcare we might unlock most of its current struggles. I said the *wisdom* of music; that does not mean a musician per se.

Shyness, lack of interest and arrogance

Let's make that personal: you should not trust me because I know how to play the piano, but because of how you see me hold that situation (or not at all).

The same Boston Medical Center lobby. The same exact day and moment as the one in our Nubian queen story could be met so differently.

> ***Shyness*** would say: "I can't. I don't know her. It could be dangerous to leap like that."

> ***Lack of interest*** would say: "The lobby was crazy—so much noise! Some woman came and said something like: *p…n-o.* I don't know; it might be something in her own language. Will Google that later."
>
> And finally, ***arrogance*** would say: "The lobby had too many people and it was not properly designed. They brought a piano in the middle, but the truth is that you cannot play a note there. Why should you? No one will hear a thing. Furthermore, no one seems to actually really care about that. They are so busy. I went back to my practice room. It seemed a better use of my time."

Shyness doubts; lack of interest couldn't care; and arrogance goes only as far as to fix it just to get rid of it one-minute past. They are three ways to miss the situation altogether. They represent what prevents a culture of care.

I am serious. It is best to know these three because they always show up. Do not think they are a mistake that can be thrown in the trash. They are not dumb. They have a lot of intelligence, but they use it to chicken out. And that is what needs to be flipped.

The question is: What kind of training is needed to uphold a culture of care—to see artistic skill as care? I would say, one that relies primarily on awareness and is rooted in wisdom. Skill will blossom effortlessly from that ground. Education should not behave as if skill is purely outsmarting continuity. Training is *being* in an environment where we can confidently meet our experience again and again—regardless if sipping a cup of tea, quitting our job, falling in love, dying, or any other wrong thing that could be done completely beautifully.

Conclusion

Let's be clear: music will not save healthcare. And vice versa, healthcare is not there to save music. The millions of individuals that put all their energy into music are not a problem. In the same way, there is nothing wrong with the millions of individuals that give themselves to the study and practice of caring for the health of others. But there should be no excuse for these worlds to delay their encounter. Their potential speaks undeniably loudly: If they acknowledge each other fully, their partnership will unveil a culture of care that will genuinely transform both music and healthcare.

Like an outburst of life, anything that could communicate an understanding and a celebration of being human would be immediately welcome. Call it the end of that subtle nightmare of cultural vacuums in healthcare. That said, more life should not be seen as a promised land. Issues will still be there—probably even more, because we would be less numbed out. But we will have edified a context and a shared vocabulary to relate to them: one that is not based on compulsively shutting down experience; on snatching individual and collective worthiness. That is a culture of care.

We should consider if there actually is any other opportunity to thrive as a society outside of that. The model that chooses to ignore worthiness is already burning out most of what we have and so desperately need. It solidifies inequity. It issues blank pain always swallowed by the same.

The good news is that it takes two to build a culture of care. Hospitals alone can only talk about it. And although they can produce glimpses of that, they cannot sustain them. On the other hand, if left to music alone, everything will look fine at the beginning. A few notes and some will conclude that music *did it*; that all is fixed. But the truth is that further along, when the real moment comes, and pain cries out for a safe corridor back to worthiness, *that* music will turn into nothing but a checked-out mumbling.

Music and health hold each other. I so wish for conservatories and hospitals not to ignore that. These are not antagonistic universes ever possible to reconcile. In truth, they are so close by that it takes a gigantic monumental effort to keep them apart. Enough then. Time for the best of music and of health to *bang!** in unison throughout.

Disclaimer: Iffy nostalgics will reject that for being an outrageous mistake (enough so to make it the right choice). It is indeed too late to backtrack. We need that "mistake," and we need to do it beautifully.

A culture of care awaits.

Artist Spotlight 4

Tag-Teaming

Jason Hedges

I used to do magic tricks when I was a kid. By the time I was ten years old, I became good enough at sleight of hand to get my first job—I worked at restaurants at night doing tableside magic. I made a lot of money. But by the time I became a teenager, I was tired of it—I had come to the realization that the tricks I had perfected only created the illusion of magic.

The only *real* magic I've ever experienced has been through music. Music can do all these great things. It evokes emotions that make us smile and cry. It opens people up and allows them to be expressive. And I have seen that music can literally help people do all of this, even after a brain injury like a stroke or accident, when they could not otherwise communicate at all. I have seen music heal people, first-hand.

I grew up in Gainesville, Florida and started playing rock and roll when I was 20. I loved being onstage just rocking and jamming and pumping up the audience. But when performing in local nursing homes and orphanages in Haiti, I could also see that music had a power that transcended the stage. So when a friend ended up in a coma after a bad accident, I went to play for him. And while performing in his room at UF Health Shands Hospital, I was able to witness his recovery. I have to believe that music was part of his healing.

When I started working at Shands, my role was to play music in order to humanize the hospital experience for patients, providing entertainment or distraction from their circumstances. My visits were always patient-driven—allowing the patient to navigate our time, request songs, or accept or decline a music visit. My work in this role was never goal-oriented; I simply intended to provide comfort and ease through this natural, organic engagement. That is the role of an artist in residence at Shands—we always bring everything back to the music. I often use music as a tool to engage and listen to patients as they open up, recall memories, or tell stories. But our conversations aren't open-ended, and they do not have therapeutic intentions. By focusing on the music, it allows me to steer clear of conversations or subject matter I am not comfortable with or qualified to address. When that does happen, I always redirect by offering a song.

In 2015, the artists in residence at Shands were invited to be part of a five-year, double-blind research study on music's effects on pain in emergency medicine. None of us had ever done anything like this before. We spent five years playing five-hour shifts on sporadic days. We had to proceed very scientifically—collecting data immediately following each patient interaction. It was challenging to navigate the research protocol, but we could see music's effects in real time: a patient's blood pressure went down; their heart rate slowed; they verbalized that the pain seemed to be going away; the amount of pain medicine they needed drastically declined.

While continuing my bedside work, therapists in the rehabilitation hospital began to see the need for music for people recovering from brain injuries and stroke. Word began to spread that my playing was helping people. I expanded my work and began playing in patients' rooms, hallways, restaurants, and in the gym as patients did their physical and occupational therapy.

Considering the data gathered for the music and emergency medicine study, I began to wonder whether there might be similar positive results if I were to play for the rehabilitation patients while they were doing their exercises in group therapy sessions. While we have not yet been able to scientifically measure music's effects in rehabilitation, therapists have anecdotally shared that their patients have been able to do more than they've been able to do previously, whenever I'm playing music. Feedback from therapists has included, "Wow, that was so much better. You walked three laps around instead of one. That's insane. That's so good!" First-hand comments from patients have included, "I did so much better today. I was able to stand longer. I was able to walk farther. I was able to do the exercises."

All of these experiences coalesced three years ago when I began working closely with speech therapists to support patients with aphasia. Aphasia is the loss of ability to understand or express speech, caused by a brain injury. Research has shown that singing can be used to induce speech by tapping into the uninjured parts of the brain associated with music. These areas can then be used to build new pathways for speech. When a patient is receptive to singing along and using live music as a tool for therapy, then I am often called in to become part of a team.

Musicians and therapists working together require dialogue in order to understand the patient's diagnosis, clarification about our distinct roles and actions, and a spirit of collaboration for creating a strategy for patient care. Once these parameters are defined, then the therapist and I are ready to navigate the healing process together. Now is when real magic and breakthroughs happen.

When a therapist and a musician work together, there is often a delicate and beautiful dance between the two practices, with me—my guitar, my voice, the music—serving as an interactive tool between therapist and patient. Sometimes the therapist leads, and I follow. And sometimes the therapist lets me do my thing, while she acts as a cheerleader. Together, this exploration opens up rich opportunities for collaborative healing.

How we exercise our roles often differs. The therapist may repeat activities over and over again in order to challenge the patient to progress. But when I play for a patient, there is no repetition. Although the therapist might push for more, if at any point in my work I feel as though the patient is no longer enjoying the music, I stop. Over time, I have learned when to leave a situation. If the patient has a breakthrough, I'll leave it at that. I don't keep going, because I've done my job. I've opened up something, and I don't want to push it. Although musicians in healthcare and therapists have different practices, we understand each other's methods and we respect those differences as long as it is working for the patient.

In 2018, I started working with Beverly. Beverly suffered from global aphasia due to a stroke. Since her arrival, she had showed no signs of emotion or communication and seemed unwilling to participate in her own recovery. I scheduled a meeting with Diane, the patient's speech therapist, to discuss how music could support Beverly's process of healing. Diane brought me into the speech therapy session with her.

She introduced me, saying, "Hello, Beverly, this is Jason and he's going to play some music for you." Beverly immediately locked eyes with me and my guitar. I greeted her saying, "Hello, Beverly. Would you like to hear a song?" She paused, and then nodded yes. Confident that we were off to a good start, I opened with "My Girl" by The Temptations. Before the iconic four-bar introduction was over, Beverly was tapping her hand on the wheelchair armrest. The therapist looked at me with surprise, smiled, and said, "Well, look at this!" As we approached the chorus, we saw Beverly's lips moving as if she was trying to sing along. Then tears came down her face. I immediately stopped and asked, "Beverly, is this okay? Would you like me to continue?" (This is a regular part of my practice. I need to know if the patient is okay with the emotional response.) She nodded, so we continued.

After the song, Diane and I praised Beverly through a round of applause. Then Diane suggested we try the song again, this time repeating the chorus over and over, while Diane encouraged Beverly to sing. To our surprise, Beverly was actually able to sing. Afterwards, we asked Beverly if she enjoyed the song and she said out loud, "Yes, I loved it." This was the very first verbal communication she had made since the stroke. Beverly had a great breakthrough.

With each session, using music as a tool for healing, Beverly showed great progress. After each session, Diane and I would make notes and talk about the effectiveness of our collaboration. Beverly eventually made a complete recovery. Later, she sent a letter to the hospital, saying "Music saved my life."

I truly believe Beverly's recovery was made possible because of the collaboration of the therapist and musician and a mutual respect for our different practices and skills. We are now seeing such powerful breakthroughs at the rehabilitation hospital. As we advance our work and document our observations, I feel confident we're just beginning to scratch the surface of music's potential for healing.

4 From Beguiling to Belonging

The Evolution of Musical-Medical Partnership

Sarah Adams Hoover

In this final chapter, we weave together the strands from the preceding sections to offer a vision in which musical artists are fully integrated into healthcare culture. In Chapter 1, we experienced the profound cultural shift away from classical music's Art Club into the healthcare environment. In Chapter 2, we examined the numerous ways in which musicians engage in this new landscape to offer positive distraction, stress reduction, entertainment, creative engagement, and interpersonal connection. In Chapter 3, we learned about best practices and training for the specialized skills they need to work in the hospital. Although partnership and collaboration have been touched upon throughout the preceding chapters, we now need to dive in more deeply. Simply put, music is a collaborative venture in the hospital, and musicians cannot succeed in achieving their aims without the support of other professionals within it.

Let us begin the conversation grounded in an understanding that musicians in healthcare and healthcare providers share and serve the same goal: *to create a culture of health.* In each domain, professionals can feel disconnected from meaningful human interaction. It is not the purview of this book to offer ways to "fix" the healthcare system or the culture of classical music, but instead to propose that through engagement with one another we can jointly promote a fundamental experience of health that arises out of our connection. Both domains bring essential wisdom and skill to healing. This has been brought into sharp relief recently as hospitals across the country have struggled to respond to the coronavirus pandemic.[1]

Healing is more basic and less tactical than beguiling, distracting, or entertaining. For the patient, the brusqueness of a care provider may be experienced the same way as the peppy demeanor of a visiting musician—neither seems to see her for who and how she really is, in her current condition and beyond it to the fullness of her identity. What she needs from the musician and care provider are compassion and honesty. To meet the patient where she is, musicians must understand and support the work of healthcare providers and determine how best to offer their unique contributions to the culture of care. This requires skill in collaboration.

Teaching Artists and Citizen Artists: A Relevant Model for Music in Healthcare

The majority of the training musicians receive in collaboration takes place in ensemble programs and is focused on music making. The field of teaching artistry provides relevant practical training for musicians moving into arts in health, specifically through experiences of collaboration: relationship-building with non-music professionals, integrating an asset-based mindset, and partnering across disciplines. Experienced teaching artists can also benefit from understanding how their skills are relevant and valuable in the healthcare context. We advance the cross-fertilization of these fields here by considering how experiences gained from the field of teaching artistry are useful in the healthcare context.

As defined by Eric Booth in his essay "The History of Teaching Artistry in the U.S.," a **teaching artist** is a hybrid practitioner-educator, "a practicing artist who develops the complementary skills, curiosities and habits of mind of an educator, who can effectively engage a wide range of participants in learning experiences, in, through, and about the arts."[2] Since the 1960s the discipline has grown from engagement with under-resourced schools to be inclusive of arts engagements for professional development and corporate leadership as well as in prisons/juvenile justice, and retirement communities. Music students can now take courses, apply for internships, and find off-campus jobs as teaching artists. Graduates often supplement teaching and gigging income with work as teaching artists to make a livable income. The only national study of teaching artistry found that teaching artist income does on average allow musicians to avoid non-arts work.[3] Some artists choose to specialize in teaching artistry as a career and work for symphonies, opera companies, and presenting organizations. Legacy music institution Carnegie Hall now has a Social Impact department that offers wide-ranging programs staffed by experienced teaching artists.[4]

The core work of the teaching artist is to create access to and forge meaningful connections with works of art and the creative process. These core activities are increasingly connected to a wide array of learning outcomes, depending on the context of the partnership in which the teaching artist works. But leading authors on music teaching artistry to date—Eric Booth[5] and David Wallace[6] specifically—have yet to address in depth the specialized environment of healthcare and the rich creative opportunities it presents. Moreover, the related concept of the citizen artist, a current term used to describe 21st-century artists, has not yet been connected with musicians working in healthcare environments. It behooves us to examine Booth's 2013 essay "The Citizen-Artist: A Revolution of the Heart Within the Arts" and consider it in relation to healthcare.[7]

Although most artists are "willing to enter a new community and give it their best," Booth notes that the **citizen artist**

> engages with a new community and listens, really hearing and feeling the life of that community, seeing it as full of assets to be tapped, empathetically connecting to the vitality of that community, and bringing his artistry to that connection.

Booth distinguishes this definition from a looser, more current use of the term:

> The common usage of the term "citizen artist" describes artists or artists in training who bring artistic offerings into economically stressed areas, or to groups who don't attend arts offerings for one reason or another. The impulse behind this view of citizen-artistry proposes that experiences of art (as defined by the Art Club) are good for people, and artists who provide such experiences are better American citizens for doing so.... I contend that most "outreach" is far from citizenship. Most of what I see is the activity on a tourist visa from the Art Club to visit another land, sometimes even seen as a "foreign" land. Let's not call visiting or partnership involvement by the name of citizenship, unless it is. Let's recognize and respect what a true artist citizen can be, so we can aspire to the transformative possibility this metaphor represents.[8]

Booth's insistence on the integrity of the concept of citizenship resonates strongly in the hospital. The realities of caring for sick and vulnerable people require a mindset and practice that respect hospital policies, procedures, and restrictions. In the context of life and death situations, we should interrogate the appropriateness of bringing musicians into the hospital; in what ways are their skills beneficial, and why does high-quality artistry matter? We reprise the suspicious security guard's basic question from Fernández Via's Impromptu 1: What are musicians here for? (Underneath that question and at the heart of Chapter 3: Do they know what they are doing here?) How can these two extremely dissimilar entities accomplish something jointly while retaining their unique identities? This is the question artists must ask themselves when approaching healthcare institutions to explore partnership: *How can the true needs of this hospital's patients and staff be authentically met by the true artistic capacities of the musician?*

This is not an easy question, but it is essential. It begs an examination of how we frame our approach to partnership. When we look at our potential partners—including healthcare providers, hospital staff, and patients—do we only see problems and deficiencies, or will we do the work to discover their capacities and assets? Musicians, music teachers, and administrators building programs are advised not to skip the basics of relationship-building—taking time for deep listening, honest communication, trust building, humility, and empathy. To support those in the hospital, musicians in healthcare must embody the core attributes of citizen artists in their work, which are, according to Booth, a "simple commitment to genuine respect, real interest, and heartfelt care."[9]

Building Interprofessional Relationships

In healthcare, it is imperative to build trust with a diverse array of care providers and staff: patient care representatives, patient services staff, charge/floor nurses, creative arts therapists, chaplains, Child Life specialists, housekeeping, and security, as well as departmental and hospital leadership. Successful integration of music into the environment of care will not happen without allies throughout the system, both on the ground within individual units and at the leadership level. Gaining trust occurs through listening and observing, communicating clearly about program and shared outcomes, and understanding and respecting professional roles, boundaries, and regulations.

In the complex, hierarchical ecosystem of the hospital, musicians are likely to interact with many employees. It is essential to understand their roles and support *their* work while engaging in music activities. On a daily shift in a bedside music program, for example, a musician logs in and retrieves instruments and materials at the program office, receiving information and instructions from administrative staff on the way. The musician may converse with a security guard en route to the unit to check in with a nurse manager or patient care representative. Here she receives updates on the status of patients on the list for the day and learns about additional patients to be seen. There may be more important details provided: who is lonely, who has family visiting, who has physical therapy or a medical test in the next half hour, and who is just about to be discharged. She gets the opportunity to assess the mood on the floor to determine whether the staff might appreciate a musical interlude near their workstation. She may enter the room of a critically ill patient where a family member or chaplain may request music to accompany prayer. On pediatric units, she may be called in to accompany a Child Life specialist on a bedside visit. A physician may bring her to the family waiting area to play music to celebrate a patient's discharge. Over the course of this shift, she has interacted with program administrators, a security guard, nurses and aides, patient care representatives, patients, family members, a chaplain, a Child Life specialist, and a physician. Authentic, collegial relationships with all of these people will help the musician more effectively support the shared goal of creating a culture of health.

In a lobby music program, a musician is likely to have a more public-facing role that intersects with the volunteer services, guest services, and/or public affairs offices. There will likely be interaction with volunteer way-finders or front desk staff, security guards, guests, patients, family members, and housekeeping staff, as well as healthcare providers and trainees on their way through public lobbies. It is not uncommon for hospital leadership to escort high-profile guests or admissions tour groups through the space while musicians are playing.

Deeper experiences of collaboration take place working side-by-side with therapists. Below we see UF Health Shands' artist in residence Ricky Kendall's insight into the expanded potential for care working with art therapist Amy:

> I learned invaluable lessons about the boundary lines between artist and patient and the intersecting lines that allowed for powerful collaboration with Amy. By merging our practices, we were not only able to cast a wide net of care and support for Brianna, but we were also able to provide support for the family and one another after the loss. These have been very

> important emotional landmarks in my work as an artist in the hospital. Therapists carry with them important causal knowledge regarding the well-being of those in critical circumstances while artists in residence travel light with an ability to inspire and to humanize the hospital experience. Together, these practices have the potential to amplify the holistic approach to arts in healthcare.[10]

Musicians in healthcare and music therapists each recognize the benefits of collaborating with one another. Jian-Wen Zhang et al. state that "a skilled musician may be able to use his or her knowledge of music to provide a significantly improved hospital environment when he or she receives support and advice from music therapists." Their findings suggest that "the collaboration between music therapists and musicians will expand both professionals' ability to provide live music in public areas of hospitals."[11] Helen Shoemark documents how the collective assets of the Royal Children's Hospital's music therapy team and musicians from the Melbourne Symphony Orchestra "expand the presence of music in the hospital," combining "the music therapist's knowledge of the specific needs of the patient/unit [with the MSO musicians'] music knowledge." In their study, the music therapist served as gatekeeper, establishing protocols and training "to promote safe, useful experiences for everyone involved," but Shoemark notes that "it was the exquisite skill of the orchestral musicians [that] created the vibrant success of this experience." These musicians identified that the hospital team of music therapists and healthcare providers was essential to their success, "allowing the musicians to simply be musicians, while ensuring the suitability and effectiveness of the experience for all the recipients."[12] The study resulted in the creation of practical guidelines for orienting musicians to playing in hospitals.[13]

As we saw in Chapter 2, musicians also work with physical, occupational, speech, or respiratory therapists to provide musician-assisted rehabilitative therapy. Working with a shared focus on the patient's rehabilitation goals is another way to expand music's impact. In Artist Spotlight 4, Jason Hedges shares how, in his work with stroke patients, his music making sometimes holds the key to unlocking rehabilitative progress that therapists have been struggling to help the patient achieve. His spotlight highlights the value of interprofessional care team, in which trained specialists from multiple, distinct fields collaborate on behalf of the patient, achieving greater health gains than each could individually.

Dr. Preeti Raghavan, rehabilitation medicine specialist who directs the Center of Excellence for Treatment, Recovery, and Rehabilitation at the Sheikh Khalifa Stroke Institute and Motor Recovery Laboratory at Johns Hopkins Medicine, frequently incorporates music in her clinical practice and research. Raghavan states that "music has been shown to be one of the most powerful elicitors of spontaneous motor action. It motivates people to adhere to exercise regimens, distracts attention from physical effort, and reduces perceived exertion." She also notes that

> adding music-supported therapy to the rehabilitative team can bridge the gap between function and social participation by enhancing the patient's self-efficacy. Conventional therapy focuses on restoring function, but when patients are in the zone while moving to music or making music, they may suddenly realize that they are capable of much more than they thought they were, inspiring and empowering them to do more.[14]

Music therapist Maria Chiarina Guerrero researched the collaborative treatment approach taken by Raghavan's interprofessional team at NYU Langone Medical Center.[15] One member of the team, an occupational therapist, shared with the music therapist that

> I knew that music was powerful, but watching you do your thing, how you changed the music—that's what I loved about it. It wasn't just putting on music in the background and doing something else; it was actually [using the] flowing [music to] help people with different goals and different instruments [achieve their goals]. And the [patients]—how they reacted, especially with the music that they knew: They got so excited and they *really moved!*[16]

Raghavan noted that it was impossible to determine the source of successful rehabilitative efforts in a multi-disciplinary approach:

> What is the active ingredient? Is it the therapeutic alliance? Is it the music? Is it the coming together of all of these ingredients? The music, the movement, the emotional connection, the socialization… In rehabilitation, there's no one key ingredient alone that stands out. They all come together – and if we can help them come together in a more synergistic way, then maybe *that's* what will help the patient.[17]

Healthcare interventions are undertaken by teams, and musicians working in the hospital are often integrated into these teams. The importance of being a supportive member of an interprofessional care team cannot be overemphasized. In a collaborative environment, musicians are able to achieve deeper, wider, and longer-lasting forms of care for patients and providers. Conversely, confusion about roles and practice boundaries, lack of respect, and inattention to the relationships in the work environment can make it impossible to achieve the creative and healing goals of the program. Penny Brill, violist and founder of Pittsburgh Symphony Orchestra's Music and Wellness program, advocates for a "client-based, collaborative and adaptive approach, where we listen to the patient, creatively shaping what we can each offer to meet their needs, which benefits all of us. Ideally, we learn and grow stronger in ways we all value."[18]

The Evolution of Partnership

Healthy partnerships are not static but evolve. In "The Citizen Artist: A Revolution of the Heart in the Arts," Booth outlines three types of relationships between artists and non-arts organizations in community arts settings.[19] He frames these as blind dating, steady dating, and marriage. We will use this framework to define and explore distinctly different types of relationships between musicians and healthcare partners within the hospital environment. As in life, there can be a lot of exciting dates that don't lead to marriage, and many types of partnership have their place in the healthcare context.

Blind Dating: Research and Pilots

Musicians (as well as other kinds of artists) are generally a welcome and exotic addition to the healthcare environment. Their creativity, demeanor, and manner of dress set them apart from others in the hospital. It is good for musicians to recognize their assets, and the ability to beguile is certainly one of them. To begin to get to know one another, blind dating is a good way to dip a toe into program design and to test potential partnerships. Blind date ideas could include:

- Public concerts in lobbies performed by volunteer musicians
- Bedside music played by musicians provided by organizations such as Musicians On Call[20]

- One-off musical events/performances provided by local arts institutions
- Pilot projects
- Short-term research studies incorporating music into patient care
- Yearly holiday programs
- Class performance projects offered by a local music school
- Student volunteer programs mentored by a local music school.

For these activities, training for artists is likely to be minimally structured and offered as needed. While there may be some support for initial efforts, there may not be funding to support artists in an ongoing way. Arts activities in healthcare settings sometimes begin as "heart" projects developed by individuals or organizations who execute them independently, without wide awareness or institutional support.

Engaging in exploratory experiences to bring music into healthcare is a worthwhile endeavor for music students. In the best of all possible worlds, these activities provide a pathway to expanded artistry and collaborative skills grounded in an approach adapted from **asset-based community development**, in which music is *shared with* rather than *performed at, to,* or *for* others, building upon the capacities and competences of those listening.[21] It is helpful to provide curious students and faculty with experiences that deepen their understanding of how music can be used to support healing and wellbeing. Guided activities welcome participants into a new paradigm of why and how to be an artist in environments far afield from the concert hall. Some may not return, and others may immediately experience an intuitive sense of fit, as we see in Tamara Wellons's Artist Spotlight 3.

We urge musicians making early forays into exploring new environments to proceed with respect and care. Let us be clear that good will and lofty notions about bringing the healing power of the arts to the hospital are not enough. Musicians are advised to examine their motivations and check their assumptions to avoid the "creative savior complex," as Omayeli Arenyeka points out:

> When exploring how to do good using our creative skills, it's important to recognize that doing good, as Teju Cole conveys in his article, "White Savior Industrial Complex," is so much more than the vague notion of "making a difference," and is so much more than our intentions. Even with good intentions our work

> can still cause harm, so before you explore how your creative skills can save the world, examine your objectives and your relationship to the problem, check in with the community affected, and remember that there are plenty of ways to contribute.[22]

In the hospital, insensitivity to others might not be received as a blunder or inability to connect but a breach of the medical profession's obligation to promote beneficence (acting in the best interest of the patient) and non-maleficence (attempting to do no harm). Musicians (and, likewise, medical providers) must avoid approaching patients with a "superiority complex, wherein you are the 'helper' or the 'savior,' and the people receiving your 'help' should accept it and be grateful," as Arenyeka points out. The superiority complex is deeply embedded in classical music culture, which has historically assumed that experiences with classical music are intrinsically good (e.g. uplifting, edifying) and that the "high art" of white European classical music is superior to the "low art" of popular music from other cultures and races, as Lawrence W. Levine chronicles in *Highbrow/Lowbrow: The Emergence of Cultural Hierarchy in America*.[23] The list of questions is provided in the text box "Before You Start: Preparing for a Potential Project in a Healthcare Setting" to help increase awareness of bias and to foster an asset-based approach.

Before You Start:

Preparing for a potential project in a healthcare setting

- Make an inventory of assets in hand (student musicians, faculty musicians, community musicians, courses or training in related areas, faculty mentors and advocates, departmental/institutional advocates, funding, relationships with healthcare providers, research partners, other). How might you gather these assets and build internal interest before you approach a healthcare organization?
- How will you find your healthcare partner? What is the value of music to them? How will you build trust and respect with a potential partner?
- How will you ensure that your activities and relationships are responsive to the cultures you hope to serve with your music? How can you approach with asset- rather than deficit-based thinking?
- How will you equip yourself/your artists? What will you need to learn in advance in order to empathize with voices unlike your own (patients, families, staff, healthcare providers)?

- How will you determine if music is needed or welcome in a given situation? How will you handle requests for genres/styles, activities, and presentation formats that do not immediately align with your own preferences or expertise?
- What is a reasonable scale and scope for the project? What can be managed by all involved?
- What parameters will be set up for all who participate in the experience? How will everyone be clear about what is going to happen and what their responsibilities are? How can you ensure there will be an experience of authentic collaboration?
- What end goals and outcomes do you have in mind, and how will you communicate them with all who take part? What are your partner's goals and outcomes?
- If things don't go well, what repercussions could there be for your partnering organization, patients and healthcare providers, yourself/your students, your institution, and any others who have taken part? What liability issues or concerns should be addressed up front?
- How will you plan to debrief with musicians, patients, and healthcare partners to evaluate the experience? What form of evaluation will you use? How will you assess skill development and knowledge gain in musicians?

Musicians can set up first dates for success by engaging in extensive observation and research before beginning programs: conducting interviews, making site visits and environmental assessments, evaluating early efforts, and piloting small-scale ideas. Daisy Fancourt provides detailed guidelines and clear frameworks for preparatory research in *Arts and Health: Designing and Researching Interventions.*[24] At Johns Hopkins, we spent several years gathering context information before building program. We made periodic visits to patient and family advisory councils to ask for specific feedback on sources of stress within individual units of the hospital and suggestions for musical activities that might address them. Insight gathered has been critical to effective program design. For example, in advance of designing a lobby music program, a group of Peabody Conservatory students and Baltimore high school interns spent a summer making an inventory of public spaces throughout the hospital campus, tracking space configurations and sizes, architectural surface materials, ambient noise level, traffic patterns, number of people present over several different times of day, and types of activity taking place. Information was gathered through observation and interviews with patients and family members, healthcare providers, front desk staff, and security guards. Informal conversations with patients and staff and formal interviews and surveys were part of a process to promote inclusive and diverse perspectives on the environment, based on users' experience.

Testing a program idea with a short-term, one-time pilot is a low-stakes way to proceed in the early dating process. Pilots require minimal financial commitment and short time frames. When a pilot is completed and debriefed, it is easy for either side to decide not to move forward. Pittsburgh Symphony Orchestra Music and Wellness program's *Musicians' Handbook* includes helpful questions for assessing a first program.[25] A pilot can create visibility, excitement, and collaborative energy to fuel next steps or clarify (re)directions for potential exploration. Additionally, PSO's *Arts Administrators and Healthcare Providers Handbook* is a good resource for beginning a music project or partnership with a healthcare facility.[26]

Steady Dating: Allies and Program Development

As dating continues, the relationship evolves and deepens. Artists, arts institutions, and healthcare organizations start to make plans together. A steady dating relationship may lead to:

- Identified stakeholders and allies
- Articulated internships and residencies
- Expanded programming with a published calendar of events
- Co-branded and coordinated publicity efforts
- Contracted, paid artists, and volunteer positions
- Established bedside music programs and concert series
- Institutionalized partnerships with formalized agreements
- Formalized training programs and protocols
- Identified funding sources.

Steady dating may be a step along the way to a more substantial commitment or the desired end itself, should partners want to retain their own autonomy. This is the case when arts organizations subcontract artists and take care of hiring, training, supervising, and payment on behalf of the hospital. The Creative Center at University Settlement, which has longstanding contracts with numerous New York City hospitals to provide visual arts programs, has chosen not to become part of any of the hospitals they serve in order to retain their independence.[27] This choice has consequences: Director Robin Glazer notes that her program has no ongoing budget line in the hospitals in which she places artists, and that The Creative Center is "the only arts organization that works in city hospitals that is not part of the hospital." The lack of secure multi-year funding may result in drastic program cuts and the inability to retain longstanding artists whose professional lives may be anchored around regular weekly shifts. These challenges notwithstanding, she still believes that the organization can better serve patients and artists through remaining independent of the healthcare system, given the cultural differences between the arts and healthcare, and the hard-driving, bottom-line approach prevalent in the healthcare industry. She has worked hard to support the organization's artists by providing compensation and benefits commensurate with other teaching artist organizations in New York.[28]

The Creative Center's institutional independence does not preclude deep collaboration. Glazer underscores that constant relationship-tending and network-building within a hospital are essential for successful partnerships. In order for the creative work to make an impact on the healthcare environment, an investment in relationship-building is essential, Glazer says. Even small things like a handmade card for a nurse's new baby can make all the difference. Although The Creative Center does not employ musicians, their handbook for visual artists, *Artists-in-Residence: The Creative Center's Approach to Arts in Healthcare*, is a useful reference.[29]

Marriage: Integration and Belonging

As a partnership matures, artists see themselves belonging in the culture of the hospital. They are not exotic curiosities or free-spirited renegades. As insiders, they participate collaboratively in the enterprise of supporting healing and making healthcare more whole. Marriage involves constant affirmation of commitment, and commitment engenders long-term and large-scale programs. Attributes of committed partnerships in the field of arts in health at established programs like Duke Health, Michigan Medicine, UF Health Shands, Houston Methodist, and Carnegie Hall include:

- Long-term partnerships and joint programs (some for over 40 years)
- Professional Artist in Residence programs and referral systems
- Concert series and lobby music programs

- Music in clinical areas (e.g. infusion centers, intensive care and surgical units, emergency departments, stroke centers)
- Musicians integrated into interprofessional care teams
- Dedicated funding, either within hospital budget or as separate philanthropic effort
- Dedicated funding and staff for research
- Ongoing programs with local arts organizations
- Partnerships with local universities
- Training and degree programs in arts in health
- Music-making activities for healthcare providers (e.g. orchestras, classes, lessons)
- Outpatient and community health programs.

One of Sarah Johnson's commitments as Chief Education Officer and Director of Carnegie Hall's Weill Music Institute has been an 11-year partnership with Jacobi Medical Center in the South Bronx. Carnegie's first steps included public concerts in auditoriums and public spaces given by a carefully selected team of teaching artists. In ongoing discussions with hospital staff, the team learned about the hospital's goals of shifting community perceptions of the facility as a place for emergency care to an understanding that Jacobi could provide essential preventive care before emergencies developed. As a result, in the second year they paired performances with health fairs to bring community members to the hospital for mammograms, vaccines, flu shots, and prenatal care. Although the concerts were designed for patients, they served the hospital's goal of getting patients in the doors for preventative care; staff discovered that musical events helped build trust between the patients and the healthcare system. Out of that experience arose a desire for in-room mini-concerts, which the musicians subsequently provided. A songwriting program for HIV-positive teenagers facilitated by a therapist in partnership with teaching artists came next. And for the past nine years, Carnegie has focused its energy at Jacobi on refining and sharing the Lullaby Project, bringing together pregnant women, new mothers, and new fathers with professional teaching artists to write, record, and perform personal lullabies with the aims of improving prenatal health and parent-child bonding.[30] Dennie Palmer Wolf's report *Being Together, Being Well* indicates that the program has positively affected health outcomes as well as perception of wellbeing and social support.[31]

The integrity of Carnegie's work with their healthcare partners stems from the collective willingness to see where things organically lead both the artists and the healthcare providers. It is worth noting that the Carnegie team has foregone other projects in order to focus deeply on the Lullaby Project, the program that seems to best align the needs of both partners. They proceed with open-mindedness, and a willing to be vulnerable, take risks, and to let go of being perceived as experts—or the stars. Johnson coaches artists to ensure that what they bring to their partners is precious, as well as a service to others. "Yes, I care about how beautifully you can play unaccompanied J.S. Bach, but I care more about how you as a human can bring Bach to other people and to meaningfully engage with them. Playing beautifully is just not enough."[32]

A Vision for the Future

Musicians and care providers are indeed already creating a culture of health together. Looking back on the past few decades alone, we see significant progress made in establishing the value of the arts as a resource for promoting health. Arts in health programs have flourished across the country at Duke, UF Health Shands, Houston Methodist, and the University of Michigan/Michigan Medicine, among others. But what's next? What do we hope for?

We envision and advocate for a future where:

All hospitals have music. Wherever they are, patients, families, and guests can expect musicians on call and music programs in place at the hospital. Hospitals provide employment for local and regional musicians and partner with local music schools to provide training for aspiring musicians in healthcare.

Music is integrated and accessible throughout the hospital environment. Music and the arts foster a culture of creativity in the midst of an environment of healing. Patients and guests look to the healthcare system to inspire creativity. They can take classes, interact and collaborate with artists, and attend or participate in concerts. Concerts provide a platform for celebrating the musical assets of the surrounding community as well as visiting artists. Music programs influence where consumers choose to go for their medical care. The hospital provides accessible, free programs for those who would not otherwise patronize the arts.

Music programs in hospitals are inclusive of and responsive to the communities, artists, and musical traditions in which the hospital is located and music schools prepare graduates with the requisite skills and mindsets to respond to local and regional hospitals' needs. Within this back-to-the-future paradigm: classical music culture embraces the value of music as service to others; expanded educational models encompass training in musical, interpersonal, and collaborative skills that equip musicians to provide accessible, interactive, inclusive music experiences in the healthcare environment; and musicians are fluent across genres, comfortable with improvisation, eager to co-create, and know how to follow their listeners. We envision a world where Art Clubs and superiority complexes are a thing of the past. Instead, there is music for all.

There is access to musical instruments and spaces for music-making across the medical campus. Pianos are unlocked and ready to be played. Volunteer and professional musicians are filling spaces with music that inspires and heals. Music rooms for patients and healthcare providers are integrated in appropriate locations throughout the facility. Instruments are available to healthcare workers to relieve stress and inspire creativity.

Music is used to support healing throughout the spectrum of care. Music is incorporated into patients' care and treatments. Music is a resource offered to patients and their families during their hospital stays. Their preferences are captured upon admission, indicating the best ways to support them during their stay. Healthcare consumers engage with music as part of their preventive care and recovery in outpatient and community health contexts through music classes and musician-supported rehabilitative therapy.

Healthcare providers prescribe music as a form of preventive or therapeutic care. Social prescribing has taken hold and arts activities are reimbursable through insurance. Music is widely recognized as fundamental to individual, community, and public health.

Arts in health is recognized as part of the allied health network of care providers. Along with music therapists, musicians in healthcare are listed as specialists within the **allied health** professions, collaborating with medical professionals and sharing "a common commitment to patient wellbeing."[33] Music is recognized within the healthcare system as a form of healing. Qualified musicians obtain training, certification, accreditation, and licensure as allied health professionals and are held to a code of ethics and standards. Licensure is contingent upon the completion of regular continuing education.

Musicians, administrators, and healthcare professionals can pursue training in arts in health. Options range from certificates to advanced professional and doctoral degrees. Arts in health training programs prepare artists, arts administrators, researchers, healthcare administrators, and healthcare providers for employment in academic, clinical, and community programs and to produce research to advance the field.

Music provides support for healthcare providers in their daily work as well as their personal and professional development. Musical activities are integrated into care providers' foundational training. Onsite programs provide access to music performances and music making and learning activities to support wellbeing. Music programs demonstrably improve workplace experience, morale, mood, recruitment, and retention among staff.

Programs have secure funding. The value of arts in health programs is evident as a line item in the healthcare system's budget, or through an endowment or dedicated philanthropic effort. Program expenses are offset by cost savings in other areas due to improvements in healthcare staff performance as well as savings on patient care.

Art lives as art within the healthcare environment and professional artists partner with therapeutic approaches when appropriate. Artists retain their unique creative domains and attributes but participate as full professionals in interdisciplinary teams. Music's power for healing extends beyond comforting us with what is already familiar to stretching us beyond what we know. Music expands our experience of care and of healing.

Through interdisciplinary collaboration we create a transformed healthcare culture and a transformed arts culture. "We have a really bad culture problem in healthcare," says Nick Dawson, Executive Director of Innovation at Kaiser Permanente. "The history of constructing institutions around doctors rather than around patients and communities has resulted in environments that are hard to work in and hard to receive care in." Dawson sees a future where artists are incorporated into teams redesigning the healthcare experience to

> bring the perspective of someone who sees, hears, touches, and builds the world differently to the table. Will art, and especially music, be a major catalyst in dismantling the barrier to humanity endemic to today's healthcare culture, or will art be the result of a transformed healthcare culture?[34]

We have a culture problem in classical music and conservatory culture, too: an obsession with perfection that constricts authentic artistry; artistic shyness or arrogance stemming from a lost connection with dignity and self-worth; a fetishizing of an idealized

European tradition; longstanding and unresolved diversity and inclusion issues; anxiety about contracting markets; a public perception of diminishing relevance; the individual and collective inability to connect art music to today's world and its social challenges; and, directly to our point in this book, *an alienation from the essential health of music.*

Nina Falk, Founder and Director of A Musical Heart, traces the arc:

> When you first start studying, you fall in love with music—the beauty, richness, and depth. You follow the whole path, but the challenges of living a musician's life can interfere with the original innocence and joy. In our desire to serve the music, the search for perfection can damage our essential relationship with music. At the bedside with patients, it is a thrill to offer the refinement of even one note for a different purpose. When life is diminishing, music connects us to something larger and allows us to let go.

Through her own experience working with patients in hospice, Falk has recovered "the purity and innocence of my original love of music and brought that joy into my public performing life. We come to heal the patient, but the musician is healed as well."[35]

Penny Brill states that

> most of the world has moved past the notion that orchestras playing Western European music are the center of the universe. Okay, so what should we be doing? What are the needs we should be trying to address? Musicians need to be doing *something!*[36]

So, drawing from her experience of healing as a cancer patient and, through close collaboration with experts across health fields, she initiated a music and wellness program for her orchestra. Brill continues to share the wisdom she has gained with patients, care providers, musicians, educators, music therapists, and arts administrators.

Eric Booth reminds us of Jim Collins' advice to organizations weathering transitions in *Good to Great*:[37] when facing crisis or challenge, Booth says, "pull in, get the right people around the table, and reconnect with your core purpose. Stand firmly on your basics and experiment boldly." He suggests this means reconnecting with the fundamental reasons why there is music in the world:

"Cut to that existential place where music has served the basic needs of humankind since the second day of creation"—as a vehicle for healing, self-expression, and community-building—and "ask yourself: Am I worthy to represent the essential role that music has played throughout history to undertake the things that nothing but music can accomplish?"[38]

The answer is *yes.* We hope this book might inspire you to employ your consummate artistry, innate compassion, and boundless imagination to create experiences of healing that music alone can accomplish.

Notes

1 Many examples of artwork created during the first wave of the coronavirus pandemic have been collected in University of Florida's Center for Arts in Medicine's COVID-19 repository. See "COVID-19 Arts Response," Center for Arts and Medicine, University of Florida Center for Arts in Medicine, 2020, https://covid.response.arts.ufl.edu.

2 Eric Booth, "The History of Teaching Artistry in the U.S.: Where it Comes From, Where it Is, and Where it's Heading," Eric Booth, self-published on ericbooth.net, rev. 2020, http://ericbooth.net/the-history-of-teaching-artistry-revised-2020/.

3 Nick Rabkin, Michael Reynolds, Eric Hedberg, and Justin Shelby, *Teaching Artists and the Future of Education* (Chicago: NORC, 2011), 178, https://www.norc.org/pdfs/tarp%20findings/teaching_artists_research_project_final_report_%209-14-11.pdf.

4 "Social Impact," Carnegie Hall, The Carnegie Hall Corporation, 2020, https://www.carnegiehall.org/Education/Social-Impact.

5 Eric Booth, *The Music Teaching Artist's Bible* (New York: Oxford, 2009).

6 David Wallace, *Engaging the Concert Audience: A Musician's Guide to Interactive Performance* (Boston: Berklee Press, 2018). Wallace devotes three pages (92–94) to teaching artistry in hospitals, which includes a brief description of the Pittsburgh Symphony Orchestra's Music and Wellness program, developed by Penny Brill.

7 Eric Booth, "The Citizen Artist: A Revolution of the Heart within the Arts," Eric Booth, self-published on ericbooth.net, accessed 2020, http://ericbooth.net/the-citizen-%c2%adartist-a-revolution-of-the-heart-within-the-arts/.

8 Ibid.

9 Ibid.

10 Ricky Kendall, "Interdisciplinary Connection," UF Health Shands Arts in Medicine, University of Florida Health, 2019, https://artsinmedicine.ufhealth.org/2019/08/29/rickys-blog-post-3/.

11 Jian-Wen Zhang, Mary A. Doherty, and John F. Mahoney, "Environmental Music in a Hospital Setting: Considerations of Music Therapists," *Music and Medicine* 10, no. 2 (2018), 77.

12 Helen Shoemark, "Sweet Melodies: Combining the Talents and Knowledge of Music Therapy and Elite Musicianship," *Voices: A World Forum for Music Therapy* 9, no. 2 (2009).
13 Helen Shoemark, *Music in Health, Music to Relax and Refresh: Guidelines for Musicians Playing Music in Hospitals* (Melbourne, Australia: Music Therapy Unit, Royal Children's Hospital, 2007).
14 Preeti Raghavan, email message to author, June 14, 2020.
15 Maria Chiarina Guerrero, "Music Therapy/Upper Limb Therapy – Integrated (MULT-I) Stroke Rehabilitation: Exploring Interprofessional Collaborative Treatment" (PhD diss., New York University, 2018).
16 Ibid., 99.
17 Ibid., 93–94.
18 Penny Brill, email message to author, May 24, 2020.
19 Booth, "The Citizen Artist."
20 Musicians On Call is a national organization which pairs volunteer musicians with volunteer guides to bring live and recorded music to patients in hospitals across the country. Musicians are vetted through an application process and trained on HIPAA, infection control, and patient interaction. Engaging performers through Musicians On Call may be a helpful way to provide a "proof of concept" when considering a music program, particularly for healthcare organizations not affiliated with music institutions. For more information, see https://www.musiciansoncall.org/faq/.
21 In *Engaging the Concert Audience*, David Wallace includes a list of audience competences that may be helpful as a place to start. Wallace, *Engaging the Concert Audience* (Boston: Berklee Press, 2018), 15–16. Wallace's theoretical framework draws upon on the asset-based community development model, detailed in John P. Kretzmann and John L. McKnight, *Building Communities from the Inside Out* (Evanstan: Institute for Policy Research, 1993). Resources for understanding the difference between needs-based and asset-based approaches can be found at DePaul University's Asset-Based Community Development Institute, https://resources.depaul.edu/abcd-institute/Pages/default.aspx.
22 Omayeli Arenyeka, "How to Think Differently about Doing Good as a Creative Person," The Creative Independent, published by Kickstarter on thecreativeindependent.com, accessed August 2020, https://thecreativeindependent.com/guides/how-to-think-differently-about-doing-good-as-a-creative-person/.
23 Lawrence W. Levine, *Highbrow/Lowbrow: The Emergence of Cultural Hierarchy in America* (Cambridge: Harvard University Press, 1988).
24 Daisy Fancourt, *Arts in Health: Designing and Researching Interventions* (Oxford: Oxford University Press, 2017). See especially Chapter 5, "Conceptualizing and planning interventions," 101–124.
25 Penny Brill, Elaine Abbott, Deborah Benkovitz Williams, Gloria Mou, and Jessi Ryan, *Musicians Handbook,* https://wellness.pittsburghsymphony.org/. http://wellness.pittsburghsymphony.org/wp-content/uploads/2016/10/Musicians-Handbook_Accessible-PDF.pdf.

26 Penny Brill, Elaine Abbott, Deborah Benkovitz Williams, Gloria Mou, and Jessi Ryan, *Arts Administrators and Healthcare Providers Handbook*, http://wellness.pittsburghsymphony.org/wp-content/uploads/2016/10/Arts-Administrators-and-Healthcare-Providers-Handbook_Accessible-PDF.pdf.
27 "About Us," The Creative Center at University Settlement, accessed 2020, http://www.thecreativecenter.org/tcc/our_organization/.
28 Robin Glazer, interview with author, February 19, 2020.
29 Geraldine Herbert, Jane Waggoner Deschner, and Robin Glazer, *Artists-in-Residence: The Creative Center's Approach to Arts in Healthcare* (New York: Creative Center, 2006).
30 "The Lullaby Project," Social Impact, The Carnegie Hall Corporation, 2020. https://www.carnegiehall.org/Education/Social-Impact/Lullaby-Project
31 Dennie Palmer Wolf, *Being Together, Being Well* (Carnegie Hall Weill Music Institute, n.d.). https://www.carnegiehall.org/-/media/CarnegieHall/Files/PDFs/Education/Social-Impact/Lullaby-Project/Lullaby-WolfBrown-Being-Together-Being-Well-Rev2020.pdf?la=en.
32 Sarah Johnson, interview with author, March 9, 2020.
33 "Allied Health Professionals," American Medical Association, American Medical Association, accessed 2020, https://www.ama-assn.org/delivering-care/ethics/allied-health-professionals.
34 Nick Dawson, interview with author, February 25, 2020.
35 Nina Falk, interview with author, September 30, 2020.
36 Penny Brill, interview with author, March 7, 2020.
37 Jim Collins, *Good to Great* (New York: HarperBusiness, 2001).
38 Eric Booth, interview with author, February 25, 2020.

Bibliography

"About Us." The Creative Center at University Settlement. Accessed 2020. http://www.thecreativecenter.org/tcc/our_organization/.

"Allied Health Professionals." American Medical Association. American Medical Association. Accessed 2020. https://www.ama-assn.org/delivering-care/ethics/allied-health-professionals.

Arenyeka, Omayeli. "How to Think Differently about Doing Good as a Creative Person." The Creative Independent. Published by Kickstarter on thecreativeindependent.com. Accessed August 2020. https://thecreativeindependent.com/guides/how-to-think-differently-about-doing-good-as-a-creative-person/.

Booth, Eric. "The Citizen Artist: A Revolution of the Heart within the Arts." Eric Booth. Self-published on ericbooth.net. Accessed 2020. http://ericbooth.net/the-citizen-%c2%adartist-a-revolution-of-the-heart-within-the-arts/.

———. "The History of Teaching Artistry in the U.S.: Where it Comes From, Where It Is, and Where it's Heading." Eric Booth. Self-published on ericbooth.net. Rev. 2020. http://ericbooth.net/the-history-of-teaching-artistry-revised-2020/.

———. *The Music Teaching Artist's Bible.* New York: Oxford, 2009.

Brill, Penny, Elaine Abbott, Deborah Benkovitz Williams, Gloria Mou, and Jessi Ryan. *Arts Administrators and Healthcare Providers Handbook.* http://wellness.pittsburghsymphony.org/wp-content/uploads/2016/10/Arts-Administrators-and-Healthcare-Providers-Handbook_Accessible-PDF.pdf.

———. *Musicians Handbook.* https://wellness.pittsburghsymphony.org/. http://wellness.pittsburghsymphony.org/wp-content/uploads/2016/10/Musicians-Handbook_Accessible-PDF.pdf.

Collins, Jim. *Good to Great.* New York: HarperBusiness, 2001.

"COVID-19 Arts Response." Center for Arts and Medicine. University of Florida Center for Arts in Medicine. 2020. https://covid.response.arts.ufl.edu.

Fancourt, Daisy. *Arts in Health: Designing and Researching Interventions.* Oxford: Oxford University Press, 2017.

Guerrero, Maria Chiarina. "Music Therapy/Upper Limb Therapy – Integrated (MULT-I) Stroke Rehabilitation: Exploring Interprofessional Collaborative Treatment." Diss. New York University (2018).

Herbert, Geraldine, Jane Waggoner Deschner, and Robin Glazer. *Artists-in-Residence: The Creative Center's Approach to Arts in Healthcare.* New York: Creative Center, 2006.

Kendall, Ricky. "Interdisciplinary Connection." UF Health Shands Arts in Medicine. University of Florida Health. 2019. https://artsinmedicine.ufhealth.org/2019/08/29/rickys-blog-post-3/.

Kretzmann, John P., and John L. McKnight, *Building Communities from the Inside Out.* Evanstan: Institute for Policy Research, 1993.

Levine, Lawrence W. *Highbrow/Lowbrow: The Emergence of Cultural Hierarchy in America.* Cambridge: Harvard University Press, 1988.

"The Lullaby Project." Social Impact. The Carnegie Hall Corporation. 2020. https://www.carnegiehall.org/Education/Social-Impact/Lullaby-Project

Rabkin, Nick, Michael Reynolds, Eric Hedberg, and Justin Shelby. *Teaching Artists and the Future of Education.* Chicago: NORC, 2011. 178. https://www.norc.org/pdfs/tarp%20findings/teaching_artists_research_project_final_report_%209-14-11.pdf.

Shoemark, Helen. *Music in Health, Music to Relax and Refresh: Guidelines for Musicians Playing Music in Hospitals.* Melbourne, Australia: Music Therapy Unit, Royal Children's Hospital, 2007.

———. "Sweet Melodies: Combining the Talents and Knowledge of Music Therapy and Elite Musicianship." *Voices: A World Forum for Music Therapy* 9, no. 2 (2009).

"Social Impact." Carnegie Hall. The Carnegie Hall Corporation. 2020. https://www.carnegiehall.org/Education/Social-Impact.

Wallace, David. *Engaging the Concert Audience: A Musician's Guide to Interactive Performance*. Boston: Berklee Press, 2018.

"What is Allied Health?" The Association of Schools Advancing Health Professions. 2020. https://www.asahp.org/what-is.

Wolf, Dennie Palmer. *Being Together, Being Well.* Carnegie Hall Weill Music Institute, n.d. https://www.carnegiehall.org/-/media/CarnegieHall/Files/PDFs/Education/Social-Impact/Lullaby-Project/Lullaby-WolfBrown-Being-Together-Being-Well-Rev2020.pdf?la=en.

Zhang, Jian-Wen, Mary A. Doherty, and John F. Mahoney. "Environmental Music in a Hospital Setting: Considerations of Music Therapists." *Music and Medicine* 10, no. 2 (2018): 77.

Glossary

All terms without citations are the authors' own definitions for the purposes of this book.

Aesthetic experience (Chapter 3)

- A "philosophical concept that explores transcendent experiences outside of religion, and often with art and nature"[1]

Allied health (Chapter 4)

- Care providers other than doctors, nurses, dentists, and pharmacists who have complementary training and expertise and who, with medical professionals, "share a common commitment to patient well-being"[2]

Artistry (Chapter 1)

- The consummate skillset of the artist that has the potential to reveal meaning, to surprise, and to delight

Arts in health (Chapter 1)

- An "interdisciplinary field dedicated to using the power of the arts to enhance health and well-being in diverse institutional and community contexts"[3]

Arts in healthcare (Chapter 1)

- A sub-field of arts in health specific to arts programs in clinical contexts, including hospitals, outpatient clinics, and healthcare units in residential facilities

Artist in residence (Chapter 2)

- A bedside musician embedded within the healthcare team or a performer/ensemble who performs regularly in lobbies or other public spaces, each with a practice developed over frequent, regular shifts

Asset-based community development (Chapter 4)

- A bottom-up approach to working in community that builds upon capacities and competences rather than deficits and problems

Attuned performance (Chapter 2)

- A highly specialized form of musical performance or accompaniment that is responsive to late-stage disease and the active dying process; a practice within music for transition

Bedside music (Chapter 2)

- Live musical performances, interactions, or activities that take place in patient rooms for individual patients, their families, and caregivers

Citizen artist (Chapter 4)

- An artist who "engages with a new community and listens, really hearing and feeling the life of that community, seeing it as full of assets to be tapped, empathetically connecting to the vitality of that community, and bringing his artistry to that connection"[4]

Collaborative composition (Chapter 2)

- Musical activity in which a trained musician facilitates a composition project with others who may or may not have musical background

Compassion fatigue (Chapter 3)

- An experience of exhaustion caused by caring for others that occurs in medical providers and caregivers

Delighter (Chapter 3)

- An unexpected element in healthcare that exceeds users' expectations and drives the growth of the hospital's business

Do no harm (Chapter 3)

- An ethical principle observed by doctors that posits the importance of minimizing harm in the pursuit of treatment

Excellence (Chapter 1)

- Impeccable technique and artistry in rendering a body of repertoire as well as a highly developed awareness of context, ability to engage with listeners, and expertise in catalyzing personally meaningful experiences with music

Flow state (Chapter 3)

- A "state or experience in which individuals are fully involved in the present moment" and may experience a merging of action and awareness[5]

Interprofessional care team (Chapter 3)

- A group of professionals from varied disciplines who collaborate in a team-based approach to provide integrated care

Live preferential music (Chapter 3)

- Music that is selected, based on preference, by the listener and is performed live by a musician

Medical humanities (Chapter 2)

- An interdisciplinary academic field that connects the health professions with other disciplines in the humanities, including the performing arts, for the purposes of improving healthcare training, practices, and culture

Music for transition (Chapter 2)

- A specialized practice of playing for patients during end-of-life care, frequently in a hospice setting

Musician in healthcare (Chapter 1)

- A professional musician who has a high level of knowledge, skill, and experience associated with both the music and healthcare domains

Musician-supported rehabilitative therapy (Chapter 2)

- Musical performance and activities provided by a live musician that offer motivation and diversion to facilitate therapists' rehabilitative goals for patients

Music making and learning (Chapter 1)

- Informal, bespoke, non-sequential skill training taking place in group or individual contexts in the hospital

Music medicine (Chapter 2)

- The intentional use of recorded music facilitated by care providers in a hospital setting with the aim of helping patients manage symptoms and influence mood

Music therapy (Chapter 1)

- The "clinical and evidence-based use of music interventions to accomplish individualized goals within a therapeutic relationship"[6]

Patient-preferred music (Chapter 2)

- Recorded or live musical selections chosen by the patient, either through requesting specific works or selecting a preferred genre, style, or mood

Personalized playlist (Chapter 2)

- The creation of a collection of a patient's favorite musical recordings to support wellbeing and symptom management, which can be facilitated by a caregiver, friend or family member, music therapist, or bedside musician

Physician-musician (Chapter 2)

- A doctor with a high level of musical training who has a deep knowledge of and appreciation for music and may be actively engaged in regular music making and performance

Positive distraction (Chapter 2)

- A "nontoxic event or stimulus" in the environment that "elicits positive feelings and holds attention without taxing or stressing the individual, thereby blocking worrisome thoughts"[7]

Professional (Chapter 1)

- A musician with a high level of skill and artistry who earns a living by working as a performer, studio teacher, music educator, teaching artist, or combination of any of these

Professionalism (Chapter 3)

- The musician's ability to make decisions, behave, and interact in ways that are expected of all those working in the healthcare environment

Self-transcendence (Chapter 3)

- The "capacity to expand self-boundaries"[8]

Skill (Chapter 1)

- The knowledge, training, and experience to repeatedly perform musical tasks with reliable results

Soundscape design (Chapter 2)

- Acoustic and musical interventions applied in a hospital setting to reduce and change the perception of clinical noise for the purposes of relieving stress and enhancing the healthcare environment

Teaching artist (Chapter 4)

- A "practicing artist who develops the complementary skills, curiosities and habits of mind of an educator, who can effectively engage a wide range of participants in learning experiences, in, through, and about the arts"[9]

Wellness music (Chapter 2)

- Digital music applications, platforms, and streaming services that invite users to curate and create personal sound environments to foster wellbeing, influence mood, and relieve stress

Notes

1 Richard Shusterman, "The end of aesthetic experience," *The Journal of Aesthetics and Art Criticism* 55, no. 1 (2010): 29–41. See also Noel Carroll, "Aesthetic experience revisited," *The British Journal of Aesthetics* 42, no. 2 (2002): 145–168.
2 "Allied Health Professionals," American Medical Association, American Medical Association, accessed 2020, https://www.ama-assn.org/delivering-care/ethics/allied-health-professionals.
3 National Association for Arts in Health, *Arts, Health, and Well-Being in America* (San Diego: National Organization for Arts in Health, 2017), https://thenoah.net/wp-content/uploads/2019/01/NOAH-2017-White-Paper-Online-Edition.pdf.
4 Eric Booth, "The citizen artist: A revolution of the heart within the arts," Eric Booth, self-published on ericbooth.net, accessed 2020, http://ericbooth.net/the-citizen-%c2%adartist-a-revolution-of-the-heart-within-the-arts/.
5 Mihaly Csikszentmihalyi, Sami Abuhamdeh, and Jeanne Nakamura, "Flow," in *Flow and the foundations of positive psychology* (Berlin: Springer, 2014), 227–238.
6 "What is music therapy?" American Music Therapy Association, American Music Therapy Association, 1998–2020, https://www.musictherapy.org/about/musictherapy/.
7 Debajyoti Pati, "Positive Distractions," Healthcare Design, Emerald X, March 11 2010, https://www.healthcaredesignmagazine.com/trends/architecture/positive-distractions/.
8 P. G. Reed, "Theory of self-transcendence," *Middle Range Theory for Nursing*, 3 (2008): 105–129.
9 Eric Booth, "The History of Teaching Artistry in the U.S.: Where it comes from, where it is, and where it's heading," Eric Booth, self-published on ericbooth.net, rev. 2020, http://ericbooth.net/the-history-of-teaching-artistry-revised-2020/.

Index

Note: *Italic* page numbers refer to *figures*.